Why I Am A Baptist

Reflections on Being Baptist in the 21st Century

Why I Am A Baptist

Baptist

Reflections on Being Baptist in the 21st Century

Cecil P. Staton Jr., editor

SMYTH&HELWYS
PUBLISHING, INCORPORATED   MACON, GEORGIA

Smyth & Helwys Publishing, Inc.
6316 Peake Road
Macon, Georgia 31210-3960
1-800-747-3016
©1999 by Smyth & Helwys Publishing
All rights reserved.
Printed in the United States of America.

Cecil P. Staton, Jr., editor

The paper used in this publication meets the minimum requirements of
American National Standard for Information Sciences—Permanence of
Paper for Printed Library Materials.
ANSI Z39.48–1984. (alk. paper)

Library of Congress Cataloging-in-Publication Data

 Why I am a Baptist:
  reflections on being Baptist in the 21st century/
  Cecil P. Staton, Jr., editor.
  p. cm.
  Includes bibliographical references.
  1. Baptists—Doctrines. 2. Baptists—Membership.
  I. Staton, Cecil P.
  BX6331.2.W48   1999
  286—dc21   99-23931
                CIP

ISBN 1-57312-290-4 (hdbk.)
ISBN 1-57312-291-2 (paper)

For
Edith White Hughes
and
Shirley Hughes Staton
with gratitude and love
for the gifts of a deep and abiding faith
and a lasting spiritual heritage

Contents

Acknowledgments

The book you now hold in your hands is the result of the work of many individuals over a period of more than one year. It occurred to me early in 1998 that a volume of essays written by Baptist leaders, presenting their understanding of and commitment to the Baptist heritage, might be a valuable historical tool as we prepare for the new millennium. What insight from our generation might be worth preserving for a new century, particularly given the controversy many Baptists have known over the last twenty years? It seems an appropriate time for reflection.

I am enormously grateful to the twenty-six contributors who agreed to share their reflections on the topic, "Why I am a Baptist." Here you will find a delightful diversity of voices, each convinced that the Baptist heritage offers an important contribution and a lasting legacy.

I am also very grateful to the staff at Smyth & Helwys for their assistance in preparing this book for publication. I am fortunate in having a gifted and dedicated staff. In particular I wish to thank Jackie Riley of the editorial department for her diligent work in preparing the manuscript. The jacket and internal design are the results of Jim Burt, Art Director, and his talented staff who always do a superb job.

Finally, I express sincere gratitude to my assistant, Amelia Barclay, CPS, who gave significant time to organizing the complicated process that brings such a book to publication, and for carefully reviewing and editing each contribution. No one could have a more professional and capable assistant.

Introduction

As the reader, you deserve to know something about the editor and the purpose of this book. As the old song goes, "It began on the morn of the day that I was born, when the cradle roll added my name." The cradle roll, of course, was the nursery of the local Baptist church.

I am Baptist born and Baptist bred. My parents, grandparents, and great-grandparents were all Baptists. I professed faith in Christ and was baptized in a Baptist church at the age of eight. I was licensed to preach at the age of seventeen, ordained a Baptist minister at the age of nineteen, graduated from a Baptist college, finished two masters degrees at a Southern Baptist seminary, and lived in a Baptist community at the University of Oxford while working on the Doctor of Philosophy degree. I have been a member of seven Baptist churches in my life in three states and two countries. It would be hard to be more Baptist than I am. But why ask twenty-six persons to contribute to a book called, "*Why I Am a Baptist*"?

I conceived of the idea for this book some months ago while reflecting upon the remarkable changes in Baptist life in the United States over the last two decades of the twentieth century. To be honest, I try not to think about that much anymore. I belong to the group that lost the struggle for the soul of the Southern Baptist Convention. We were defeated, or so we thought at first. Now some of us think we actually won by leaving behind what had become for many an idol. But that will not make much sense unless you were along for the journey. You will be grateful to know that a rehashing of that struggle is unimportant for the purposes of this book; it is readily available elsewhere.[1] I confess, however, that the results of the controversy provide much of the motivation for this book, which derives from a deep personal concern for the future of the Baptist identity. Why?

One may agree or disagree with the direction Baptist life has taken in the last two decades, but one cannot disagree with the fact that the Baptist identity has been totally reshaped for the foreseeable future by the twenty-year-old fundamentalist/moderate controversy within the largest Protestant denomination in America, the Southern Baptist Convention.

All Baptist groups in America—north, south, black, white—have been influenced by this controversy whether or not they wished to be. This controversy has not only overshadowed the Baptist landscape, but it has also seized the popular fascination with and understanding of Baptists by others.

The Baptist identity in America is now largely conceived of in terms of the faces and voices of persons such as Jerry Falwell, Charles Stanley, Paige Patterson, Richard Land, and Al Mohler—all representatives of one side of the controversy. Consider the fact that these individuals have become the voices that interpret the Baptist identity for the media, secular society, and many Christians who are not Baptist. They are the "Baptist" faces you see on the "Today Show," "Larry King Live," and similar programs that address issues related to religion in American culture and in particular Baptist responses to such issues as secularism, family, the role of women, abortion, and homosexuality.

Of course, there are other "Baptist" faces and voices that influence popular perceptions of the Baptist identity to a lesser degree. The political side of American life has been filled with Baptists in recent years. Bill Clinton, Al Gore, Newt Gingrich, Trent Lott, and Strom Thurmond are all Baptists. These, however, rarely speak directly to their "baptistness," and their images and rhetoric surely contribute to the confusing fog surrounding the Baptist identity at this juncture in history. Jimmy Carter, a lifelong Baptist, has been a voice of hope and reason for many who have been more proud to be a Baptist because of his faith and personal commitments. Tony Campolo is a significant Baptist voice who has offered an alternative to the shrill chorus of prominent ultraconservative Baptist leaders. Countless other Baptist leaders struggle to be heard; but with less availability to media exposure, they rarely succeed.

Let us be honest. No one has a copyright on the word "Baptist," and thus anyone can call himself or herself a Baptist. The Baptist emphasis on the priesthood of all believers, or the right of individuals to read and interpret scripture for themselves, encourages multiple voices, opinions, and views. With honor or shame, theological and political conservatives, moderates, and liberals all continue to wear the name "Baptist." But something has changed in recent years.

Some lifelong Baptists are now ashamed to be known by that name. This is perhaps most evident in the recent phenomenon of more and more churches, both conservative and progressive, dropping the word Baptist from their names. For some, it is now downright embarrassing to be identified as "Baptist." I confess I feel this way all too often. "Baptist" has become a word that in the popular culture connotes arrogance and ignorance and in some circles brings ridicule and derision. Baptists are stereotypically conceived by many as ignorant, mostly southern Christians who would rather fight over seemingly unimportant issues than make a genuine difference in a world of great need.

Yet surely there is another side to Baptist life that has been hidden from view by the results of the controversy. Surely there is more to being "Baptist" than this. There are important aspects of the Baptist identity that have been overshadowed by the clouds of controversy. It is as though a beautiful mountain range has been permanently lost from view by a cloud cover that will not retreat.

Again, the purpose of this book is not to focus on the controversy or to cast stones at certain members of the Baptist family with whom some of us may disagree. The Baptist tent is a large one indeed. Rather, the purpose is to give voice to that which is good and honorable about the Baptist identity. The method chosen is a collection of "Baptist" voices speaking out at the end of one century and the beginning of a new millennium in order to bring to light and to celebrate those things about the Baptist vision that are positive, relevant, and important.

This book reflects one modest attempt to capture what is best about Baptists by giving voice to the reflections of twenty-seven leaders in Baptist life today. No attempt has been made to blend the voices you will hear in this book. You will find distinct voices from Baptists in the South, some happily connected to the SBC and others no longer in that fold. You will hear the voices of Baptists from the North (American Baptist Churches), male and female voices, African-American voices, European voices, and even the voice of a former President of the United States. None was told what to write. They were simply asked to offer their response to the declaration "Why I am a Baptist," and happily they did. Their responses are recorded here in the hope that we may celebrate what is best about the Baptist heritage, reclaim it, and preserve it for a new generation.

Of course, it is ultimately up to the reader to decide whether or not this book is significant or relevant. I believe it is, and I hope it will contribute in a positive way to a greater appreciation and clarification of the Baptist identity.

You deserve to know my personal prejudices as the convener of this group of voices and the editor of this book. I remain a Baptist today primarily because of my commitment to the historic Baptist vision. This vision has had a tremendous impact on the Western world since those first Baptists in the early seventeenth century, John Smyth and Thomas Helwys, dared to take a stand against a state church on the principle of religious liberty. Religious liberty is in my view the Baptist genius, and I deeply regret its being overshadowed today and the threat of its disappearing from the larger Baptist landscape.

The vision of Smyth and Helwys eventually made its way to the new world and was embodied in the life and work of Roger Williams, the founder of Rhode Island (1636), the first colony to embrace religious liberty for its citizens and to reject a state church. Later, Baptist revolutionary war patriot Isaac Backus worked diligently in the last quarter of the eighteenth century to bring about change in Massachusetts, which finally gave up its state church in 1833. One could also point to the significant influence of Virginia Baptist pastor John Leland upon James Madison, which led to the First Amendment of the Constitution in 1789: "Congress shall make no law respecting an establishment of religion or prohibiting the free exercise thereof." Baptists have stood for many things, but fundamental to the historic Baptist vision is a commitment to religious liberty. Certainly the names of others who staked their lives on the concept of religious liberty could be added to this list of heroes.

The bottom line for me, then, is that there is a side to Baptist life that is in danger of being forgotten, or at least pushed well into the shadows. This is wrong. The Baptist heritage with its emphasis upon religious liberty and the priesthood of all believers has played a significant role in the history of this country. Although anyone can call himself or herself a Baptist, and anyone who can gain the media's attention can shape the popular perception of Baptists, it is important that the heritage of the Baptist identity not be lost, forgotten, or abandoned.

Listen, then, in the pages of this book for Baptist voices, voices of hope and concern. You will hear a choir of dissonant voices, yet voices that blend to speak out of the hope and promise of a great tradition that may yet offer a fresh and relevant voice to the twenty-first century.

Note

[1]See, for example, Grady C. Cothen, *What Happened to the Southern Baptist Convention? A Memoir of the Controversy* (Macon GA: Smyth & Helwys, 1993); Grady C. Cothen, *The New SBC: Fundamentalism's Impact on the Southern Baptist Convention* (Macon GA: Smyth & Helwys, 1995); and Walter B. Shurden, ed., *The Struggle for the Soul of the SBC: Moderate Responses to the Fundamentalist Movement* (Macon GA: Mercer University Press, 1993).

—Cecil P. Staton, Jr.
Macon, Georgia
Easter 1999

Still a Baptist

—— *Jimmy R. Allen* ——

The issue I face in these days of turmoil and the ascendancy of fundamentalism in the leadership of the Southern Baptist Convention is
not so much why I am a Baptist as it is why I am *still* a Baptist.

The image with which I must contend is that Baptists are a people
of harsh judgmentalism, cold-hearted rejection of people over minor
matters of biblical interpretation, bent on centralizing of power and
developing creedalism of conformity. Yet I am still a Baptist. But I am
not still a Baptist because we have unique beliefs.

Catalytic experiences are easily remembered. There are those times
when things come together and hang on in memory. One of those
times occurred when I was finishing my theological education. I was
invited to attend a meeting on ethics and international relations con-
vening in New York City. It was my first visit to that city. At the meeting
heavy discussions were held on the issues of nuclear warfare, peace
efforts, public policy, and the demands of Christian ethics. However,
the week stands out not for the discussions, but for a discovery about
my Baptist identity.

One of the participants, a chaplain at an eastern university, was
also in New York City for his first time. We utilized every minute of free
time to see as much as we could in the city. As we visited places we had
always heard about, we talked about the values that drove us. It was my
first encounter with a real live and convinced liberal. He challenged me
at every turn in the theological road. I responded in kind. By the end of
the week he was suggesting that we write a book about conversations
between an unapologetic liberal and an unreconstructed conservative!
The book was never written, but the experience was never forgotten.

What I discovered was that Baptists have no unique doctrines unparalleled in the belief systems of others. As I ticked off the combination of beliefs that caused me to be a Baptist, my new friend was quick to point out that this tradition or that one had similar beliefs. The difference became apparent. We have no copyright on soul freedom and religious liberty, rejection of creedalism, necessity of personal experience with God in a new birth, immersion witness in believer's baptism, urgent missionary impulse, congregational form of church government, authority and inspiration of scripture, priesthood of the believer, and the Lordship of Christ. The uniqueness about us is the combination of those ideas and teachings. The other major difference is the passion with which we center in on soul freedom and individual access to God under the lordship of Jesus Christ.

I am still a Baptist because I find no other group that clusters these teachings as close to the New Testament message as do the people called Baptists. Also, I am still a Baptist because the Baptist movement is larger than its fundamentalist element.

One factor in my capacity to stay a Baptist is that I was inoculated against fundamentalism at a very early age. It equips me to recognize the virus and reject it as an aberration in an otherwise healthy body. I also learned an appreciation for the legitimate role of fundamentalism in the overall health of the body of believers.

I grew up in Dallas, Texas. The church house in which I lived in my childhood was constructed by J. Frank Norris, the founder of the Baptist fundamentalist movement. He built the church when he was in good standing with mainstream Baptists and before his radical commitment to conformity to creedalism caused his ejection from the Texas Baptist Convention. In that same metropolitan area John R. Rice was a pastor. His fighting spirit for fundamentalism made him a partner and then a competitor with Frank Norris. In his generation he was to become one of fundamentalism's major voices. As a child, I learned of the weekly hate telegrams intercepted by the deacons of First Baptist Church of Dallas as Frank Norris poured out his hostility on George W. Truett, their pastor and one of my early heroes.

I discovered early that fundamentalists are legalists in the heritage of passionately committed Pharisees of the first century. They are often good people, capable of generosity, care, and genuine service. The problem is that they live in a straight-line, propositional world. When life gets outside the lines, they become angry, disturbed, and punishing. Baptists are not the only people who have them. History leaves us a tragic picture of John Calvin standing and watching a believer by the name of Michael Servetus burn at the stake because he wanted to take the simple Bible language as authoritative instead of Calvin's construction of it. Jesus had vivid things to say about Pharisees.

Viruses in the body sometime serve a good purpose of keeping the immune system on alert. If they do not gain strength enough to invade the whole body, they contribute to the health of the whole. They become destructive, however, when they multiply to take over the body. Fundamentalism has kept Baptists on their toes and alerted them to the crucial importance of biblical authority and to the fact that cooperation with other Christians is accomplished in coordinated activity without watering down our convictions to gain common language about God.

When the virus got out of control in Southern Baptist life, it was because fundamentalism married secular political methods within the Convention's decision making. When fundamentalism gets 51 percent of the vote, the gears shift. There is no room for dissenters to assist in formulating decisions. The virus has become a sickness.

The challenge for my staying in the Baptist movement includes the question of what you do with a sick body. Do you seek to deal with the virus and regain health, or do you abandon the sick to shrivel and die?

Another factor that draws me to stay in the Baptist movement is the intensity with which we give ourselves to the mission. Local congregations are still the center of mission endeavor.

When I was eight years old, my father left his insurance job in Dallas to accept God's call to preach. He found a neighborhood in the inner city in which a Baptist church had moved out in an early experience of "white flight." I was included in the prayerful decision. We moved in to share Christ in that neighborhood.

No external support system existed. Our support came from God who revealed His immediacy and our access to Him. Vivid in my memory is the day we gathered around the breakfast table and Dad said,

"We have nothing to eat today and no money to get something. I want us to pray that God will provide." Then he asked my mother, "Darling, do you believe in prayer?" She replied, "Yes I do." I thought the question curious. He turned to me and said, "Jimmy, do you believe in prayer?" "Yes, sir, I do." "Then we are going to ask God to give us some food today. " Each of us voiced our prayer.

In the middle of the morning a young woman who worshiped with us came to the door with a pound of pinto beans. Evelyn Taft said, "I have this pound of beans and no place to cook them." My mother cooked them. Evelyn joined us in a meal in which I discovered that God sometimes answers prayer with a bag of beans! It became formative in my understanding that we have direct and personal access to God. Later I learned to call it the "priesthood of the believer."

While there was no ecclesiastical structure to support us at that time, there was also none to prevent us from that venture. Risk-taking faith in meeting the needs of the people for whom Christ died was magnetic in my life. We were part of an urgent enterprise to share the good news in a mission to the whole world. The priority was missions. I soon learned that our little congregation had equal voice in the work of the associations of Baptists with whom we cooperated. It was an early lesson in the value of grass-roots democracy and the conviction that the Holy Spirit guides believers in a congregational theocracy. Baptists are the products of that missionary impulse. It is worth preserving. In addition to the centrality of mission, I am still a Baptist because of the commitment to soul freedom and religious liberty.

Baptist scholar Emmanuel Carlson, then serving as Executive Director of the Baptist Joint Committee on Public Affairs, helped me to understand that religious liberty and separation of church and state are not simply an arrangement for freedom of expression for religion. These concepts are not based on rendering to Caesar what is Caesar's and to God what is God's. They are born in the very nature of creation and first revealed in the garden of Eden. They are the refusal of God to coerce the human response to God's loving offer. While humans must be responsible for the consequences of their decisions, they make their decisions by the very nature of the religious experience. To the degree that coercion enters into the process, religious response is weakened and thwarted. God made us free *and* responsible.

The story of America's development of the structures of separation of church and state is filled with the Baptist understanding of soul freedom. From Roger Williams to John Leland and his dealings with James Madison about the Bill of Rights, Baptists take pride in our role in issues of freedom of religion. Even in the complexity of the welfare state we have impacted processes far more effectively than our numbers can explain.

Despite the manner in which some Baptists are abandoning the idea, trusting truth to win is a capstone of a Baptist view of life. It is the belief that the Holy Spirit does indeed guide us into all truth. It is the confidence that Jesus is "the Way, the *Truth*, and the Life."

The greatest challenge to my being "still a Baptist" does not lie in formal relationships. It is easy to maintain my relationship with a Baptist congregation that reflects the convictions of mainstream Baptists. The challenge is to deal with inner spiritual attitudes as I see unbaptistic Baptists controlling institutions, speaking as if they represent someone other than themselves and contributing to the denigration of Baptists in the minds of the general public. My life and that of my family has taken turns that have made me often revisit the book of Job. It was a profound moment when I rediscovered that Job did not recover from his woundedness until the moment when he prayed for those who had done the wounding.

Baptist Born, Baptist Bred

—— *Robert C. Ballance, Jr.* ——

Almost fifteen years ago a close friend of mine—a Methodist —had asked his pastor, who was soon to be away on vacation, to have me, a Baptist preacher-in-the-making, fill their pulpit in the pastor's absence.

Because of my friend, when the invitation came from that church's minister, I gladly accepted. The Methodist church, after all, was located in my small hometown. It would be good to return for a visit.

When the service was over, this is what my friend said to me: "Why are you a Baptist anyway? You sound just like one of our pastors." He was surprised that I did not shout and yell and speak only about hell the way he thought we Baptists all did.

I was Baptist born and Baptist bred. I had been in Baptist churches and their programs all of my life. I had attended Baptist kindergarten, two Baptist colleges, and was attending a Baptist seminary at the time. Everyone in our family on either side of the family tree was Baptist. I could even claim Charles Bray Williams, the translator of *The Williams New Testament,* as my great-great-uncle on my paternal grandmother's side. He was thoroughly Baptist, giving his life to Baptist institutions in Georgia, Texas, and Alabama. But as to why I myself was a Baptist, well I had never really given the matter any serious thought. The only answer I could come up with for my friend that day was a vacant, "Just because."

My friend's question, along with my experience that day of preaching for the first time ever in my young life from a pulpit that belonged to a tradition other than my own, provided much food for personal thought: Just why *am* I a Baptist?

In April 1995 the Center for Christian Ethics in Dallas, Texas, reprinted and made available by special request an article it had run earlier in *Christian Ethics Today*. The article's title? "Why I Am a Baptist." Its author, the distinguished Walter Rauschenbusch, had given serious thought to this question, carefully setting his answer down on paper in a series of essays nearly a hundred years earlier. The opening paragraph of those compiled essays includes this statement:

> Most men [*sic*] are Catholics or Protestants or Jews, and that's all there is of it. If the angels tonight should steal a hundred Baptist babies and replace them by Episcopalian babies, it is fair to assume that the babies which might have grown up to champion episcopacy and the apostolic succession and the Prayer Book, would learn to smile the smile of conscious superiority at those very things. There are some of us who have become Baptists from simple conviction and have had to leave the denomination of their parents to follow where truth led them. But the majority of us who are Baptists were born into Baptist families, and I am one of that majority.
>
> But that expresses only half the truth. We are Americans because we were born so. But it is our duty and our right clearly and increasingly to understand what our country stands for and to adopt as our personal principles those ideals of democracy and equality on which our national life was founded. So we are Americans by birth; but we must become Americans by personal conviction. In the same way we may be Baptists by birth, but we must become Baptists by conviction.[1]

Rauschenbusch, by the end of his lengthy but thoughtful essay series, offered this simple conclusion: "I began by being a Baptist because my father was, but today I am a Baptist because with my convictions, I could not well be anything else."[2]

In his compiled essay the professor sets forth several principles that had been distinctively and historically Baptist. His convictions I have borrowed as the starting point of my own thinking through why I am a Baptist and not something else. Though his detailed essay is well written and worthy of further study, when succinctly put, I found that for me personally Dr. Rauschenbusch's convictions could be reduced to two simple statements of belief that form the very basis for my being and remaining a Baptist: (1) Baptists emphasize the primacy of personal Christian experience, and (2) Baptists practice democracy in our organized church life.

Sensitive to the strivings of others to be followers of Christ through traditions outside the Baptist family, Rauschenbusch, the statesman that he was, acknowledged with humility his gratitude for these fellow believers. He noted, though, that these traditions go about fostering faith in ways very different than Baptists. He then used the ancestors of faith for all of us to point out the flaws that such traditions can render by reminding us of how ancient Judaism sought God with elaborate temple worship, which emphasized bloody sacrifices and faith-inhibiting laws, rules, and regulations. He then reminded us that Christ himself brought to us ways far simpler for approaching God.

The well-known father of the "social gospel" movement two generations ago then moved from a gentle consideration of other traditions to a far more poignant critique:[3]

> All religious bodies carry with them a good many clinging remnants of their childhood stage, beliefs and customs that were superstitious in their origin and never belonged to genuine Christianity. And some religious bodies have squarely refused ever to strip these things off; they cherish the remnants of heathenism as their most precious and fundamental possessions. Thus it becomes a matter of importance for an intelligent Christian to inquire where he can find Christianity in its least adulterated form.[4]

For Rauschenbusch, the Baptist tradition was that way most unadulterated and enlightened. There is danger here, however, of arrogance if one is not careful—the arrogance of believing that one has all the truth and no one else does.

In recent decades this arrogance has been illustrated most readily among Southern Baptists as certain elements within that particular brand of Baptist faith and belief continue too much to cherish wrongful remnants of belief or elevate to heights of idolatry individual and corporate convictions (i.e., belief in the inerrancy of scripture). Even the simplistic Baptist faith to which we claim to adhere can become adulterated and unenlightened when not under continual scrutiny.

Rauschenbusch remained adamant throughout life, however, that when it comes to an individual's attaining and enlarging faith, simple experience is the key. For him, neither elaborate ritual nor carefully crafted creeds would do. For his fully Baptist self, it was experience—feeling and passion for one's beliefs—that ensured freedom of religion, which served only to make one's faith ever more valuable in the eyes of the God one sought to worship and follow.

Bill Moyers, a former Baptist himself, and really still one of us, puts the same truth in his own unique way:

> At last count there are twenty-seven varieties of Baptists in this country; the brand that appeals to many of us holds that while the Bible is our anchor, it is no icon; that revelation continues, truth is not frozen in doctrine, but emerges from experience and encounter, and continuity is found in the community of faith that includes both saints and sinners. In Jesus we see the power of the living Word over tired practice and dead belief.[5]

There may be times when we Baptists—even the best among us — go overboard in clinging to this first principle. As for me, having carefully studied many of the other Christian traditions Rauschenbusch critiques, I must agree with the professor and with Moyers: faith experience over and against creed and ritual is indeed one of our greatest Baptist strengths and remains one of our greatest hallmarks.

I do, however, enjoy participating in the worship and ritual of other traditions far more complex than we Baptists have to offer. I also find the study and recital of the various creeds of other Christian traditions challenging and enlightening. But in the end I embrace wholeheartedly this notion that experience is a far more worthy means for enabling and enhancing Christian faith. Though often abused by manipulative evangelistic techniques by some overzealous Baptists among us, I still cling to the experience aspect with my whole heart and full mind.

In addition to the primacy of personal experience, Baptists uphold democracy as an ideal. It is, however, an ideal that often suffers greatly in our church meetings and in our national conventions, convocations, and assemblies. It always has and always will. Indeed, the very nature and purpose of democratic principles enable such suffering.

Rauschenbusch's sole rationale for including the practice of democracy as a Baptist distinctive, flaws and all, however, was quite simple: "Religion is not a purely individual matter."[6] It is, rather—or at least it should be—a social endeavor, calling us together into community and cooperation for the Christian cause.

True democracy, however, means that each individual is free to think for himself, free to interpret scripture for herself, free to discern the will of God for themselves. This means, therefore, that each church is a localized democracy. These local democracies, however, while allowing "ample room for those with God-given powers for leadership" to lead, hold each individual and the community fully accountable and responsible to one another and to God.[7]

It may stem from nothing more than the rebellious son in me that emerged during my formative years, a nature that seems only to grow more bold as I age, but I still do not like to be told by anyone else what I must be, believe, or do. And nowhere am I more passionate about that feeling than when it comes to faith matters. So for me, this "baptistic" principle is most appealing. In fact, popes, cardinals, bishops, and district superintendents—along with the hierarchy of any other Christian tradition—would find in me a worthy challenge were I to have to abide always by their decisions and decrees. Even the congregations I have served would say this is true of me.

The democratic principle within the Baptist Christian tradition, therefore, fits well with who I am—again, a major reason I have been and still remain a Baptist. The Baptist view of church life makes each individual a priest, whether or not ordained for service. Indeed, the act of ordination for me personally is merely an act designed to affirm one's gifts for service and not an act of administering any kind of authority as in some other Christian traditions.

The book of 1 Peter (2:5, 9) is the place most often referenced by Baptists to support this notion of an equality of priesthood of and for all believers, with Christ alone as head. Rauschenbusch, however, finds support for the universality of a priestly servanthood of all believers in the very heart of the Gospels. He cites Matthew 23:1-12 to support this notion. In this passage Jesus tells his followers that the only way to greatness is through service. The professor's conclusion regarding the kind of hierarchy found in any of the other Christian traditions is: "Jesus' word settles it for me."[8] For Rauschenbusch, then, there was no hierarchy to which any must answer but Christ and Christ himself; likewise for me.

Finally, under this reason for being Baptist—the aspect of a democratic rule in the church—Rauschenbusch lists two other principles for which Baptists historically have been the most remembered and revered: the autonomy of the local church and separation of church and state.

In fact, if one word had to be chosen to capture the historic Baptist identity, that word, according to Walter Shurden, would be "freedom."[9] And while our contemporary situation, at least in Southern Baptist circles, may cause some to question our being champions of freedom and separation of church and state, our history when objectively studied provides ample proof: freedom is our hallmark.

I yield again to Moyers, who through childhood memory illustrates poetically the freedoms and democratic principles we in Baptist life have embraced, yet often capriciously so:

> I also learned about democracy in [the Baptist church of my roots].
> It was the very embodiment of home rule. In deciding church affairs
> every believer had an equal voice. Every leader called to office—
> whether pastor, deacon, or teacher—was subject to a vote of the
> congregation; and leaders were expected to be servants, not rulers. It
> was the pew, and not the pulpit, that we thought should be exalted.
> This leveling meant that we fought a lot. My father said that Adam
> and Eve must have been the first Democrats because only Democrats
> could mess up Paradise, and he was certain that Cain and Abel were
> the first Baptists because they introduced fratricide to the Bible.[10]

Of course, with such democracy and freedom, and Shurden says as much in the same paragraph referenced above, must come responsibility.[11] Indeed, comprehending freedom and making use of it reverently and with seasoned responsibility, which includes respecting the freedom and responsible interpretations others yield, is for me at the very essence of what it means to be a true Baptist. To do otherwise is to dishonor the tradition altogether, dishonoring, too, all who have paid for this treasured possession—some with their very lives—throughout the centuries. Most of all, to dishonor our freedom and democracy in faith matters is to dishonor the very Christ we seek to worship and serve as Baptist Christians, for he gave his life for this principle first.

Therefore, embracing, honoring, and—even when necessary—willingly fighting for such freedom, is why I have been and choose to remain a Baptist.

I wish I could have had this answer ready almost two decades ago when my Methodist friend asked me, "Just why are you a Baptist anyway?" What I sensed at the time, from his questions during the meal after worship that day, was his gentle attempt to make a Methodist of me. Perhaps, however, if I had had this answer then, I might have made a Baptist of him instead!

But then I am a *true* Baptist. And as such, I cannot deny my friend *his* freedom to be what he believes is best for himself. I wish him well, therefore, as an elder in that same small Methodist church today. At the same time I am grateful for the freedom to choose, too, the tradition that is mine now and always will be. Grateful, too, for all those Baptists, past and present, who have made this the great tradition that it is. May God help us to remain faithful to the task.

Notes

[1]Walter Rauschenbusch, "Why I Am a Baptist," in *Christian Ethics Today* (April 1995): 20.

[2]Ibid.

[3]Walter Rauschenbusch, *A Theology for The Social Gospel* (Nashville: Abingdon, 1981).

[4]Rauschenbusch, "Why I Am a Baptist," 21.

[5]Bill Moyers, "On Being a Baptist," in *Best Sermons*, vol. 7 (San Francisco: Harper-Collins, 1994) 87.

[6]Rauschenbusch, "Why I Am a Baptist," 24.

[7]Ibid., 25.

[8]Ibid.

[9]Walter B. Shurden, *The Baptist Identity: Four Fragile Freedoms* (Macon GA: Smyth & Helwys, 1993) 55.

[10]Moyers, "On Being a Baptist," 86.

[11]Shurden, *The Baptist Identity*, 56.

The Cloud of Baptist Witnesses

—— Tony Campolo ——

There are those who justifiably cite "soul freedom" as that which makes being Baptist really important to them. They are individualistic free thinkers who want to belong to a church that calls for unity in essentials (i.e., that Jesus Christ is Lord, Savior, and God), accepts diversity in nonessentials, and expresses charity in all things. This Baptist distinctive has kept churches from putting their members in theological straightjackets that would keep them from working out their individual salvation with fear and trembling.

Others claim that for them the crucial and determining denominational distinctive that establishes their commitment to being Baptist is the doctrine of the autonomy of the local church. The belief that any given body of Baptist believers can make its own decisions in matters of faith and practice seems to them to be biblically sound. The call to Christians in a local setting to seek the leading of the Holy Spirit in a collective manner when decisions have to be made replicates for them New Testament Christianity. They believe that each congregation of Baptist believers has the right to determine its own destiny, free from interference from a larger body of churches or a denominational hierarchy.

For me, however, my commitment to being a Baptist has more to do with being connected to our Baptist heroes of the faith who have represented what is best about modern-day Christianity. What makes being a Baptist so important to me is that it gives me the honor of being part of a tradition that links me with three preachers who I think exemplify what Jesus has called the church to be and to do.

Centuries ago a Baptist gave birth to the modern Protestant missionary movement when William Carey, a British shoemaker, exercised
his "soul freedom" by declaring to the skeptical clergy of the North-
ampton Association of Baptist churches that God had called him to go
to India to preach the gospel. Those staunchly Calvinist preachers in
the association of Baptist churches in and around Moulton, England,
where Carey served as a lay preacher, let him know "in no uncertain
terms" that their doctrine of predestination precluded the necessity of
sending missionaries to places such as India. According to them, if God
wanted to save the "heathen" of India, God would do so without any
British Christians taking the initiative. They told Carey that he would
be running ahead of God if he went to India as a missionary, unless
there was specific evidence of the intervention of God in this venture.
But Carey was determined to go with or without their approval; as a
"soul-free" Baptist, he felt "called" to go. Fortunately, those British
church leaders eventually gave him their blessing and lent him their
support.

A direct consequence of Carey's heroic stand against the clergy of
his day was a change of consciousness about the mission of the church
not only among Baptists, but also among Christians of all denominations. Carey's commitment to the doctrine of the priesthood of all
believers led him to the conviction that the clergy had no special status
before God. He did not feel obligated to minimize his call to go to
India simply because the clergy said he ought to stay home and fix
shoes. As a Baptist, Carey refused to accept the idea that the clergy had
some special direct line to God that was inaccessible to unordained
Christians. He firmly believed that the ordained and the unordained
had equal access to God. It was not that he wanted to minimize the
ordination of the clergy. Rather, he wanted to affirm that every Christian was ordained for ministry. Because he believed that he was
ordained for ministry, Carey the shoemaker was ready to step forward
and volunteer for missionary service in India. For better or for worse,
an army of other Baptists who believed like Carey have done the same.

International missionary work is so much a part of the agenda of
contemporary Baptists that it is hard to imagine there was once a
reluctance to send out messengers of the gospel to those places where

Christ's name had never been heard. It was Carey who changed the Baptist consciousness about missions and made us into the missionary-minded people we are today. In my own ministry my primary emphasis has been to challenge young people to follow in Christ's footsteps as missionaries. Wherever I preach I call on Christians to engage themselves in the missionary enterprise, even if their service will be short-term.

It is my conviction that going out as missionaries has a transforming influence on Christians. Interacting with the poor and needy focuses those who serve to examine their own lifestyles and has led many to commit themselves to living simply so that others might simply live. Being on the mission field, even short-term, challenges people to rethink who they are, what they believe, and what the meaning of their lives ought to be. Missionary service radicalizes people into the kind of lifestyle Jesus calls us to via Scripture. There was a time when I thought that the only people who should go into missionary service were those who had had a special call from God, but I now believe there has to be a special calling from God for a person not to be a missionary.

The second giant of Baptist Christendom who has inspired me and challenged me to action is Walter Rauschenbusch. This unquestioned founder of the "social gospel" looms large in my reflections on what it means to be Christian in contemporary society. It was Rauschenbusch who lifted out of Scripture and brought to the attention of twentieth-century Christians a major theme that most had been lulled into ignoring: he reintroduced the church to the biblical message of the Kingdom of God.

Evangelical preaching in America, from Jonathan Edwards on, had made the gospel into a prescription for getting into heaven and staying out of hell. Salvation was usually limited to a penal-substitutionary doctrine of the atonement that gave believers the promise of a life after death, but did little to address the systemic evils of a society that had created extensive injustices for the poor and the oppressed. Then along came Rauschenbusch, a Baptist preacher, prophet, and theologian, who helped the church to see once more that God had sent Jesus into the world not only to change the hearts and minds of individuals, but also to transform the world into the kind of world God had created it to be. He helped a new generation of Christian activists to understand that the call of Christ was not only to get people ready for the next world, but also to invite us to join him in the task of societal transformation. Christianity, he claimed, was a call to join Christ in the work of the one who had sent him so that we can pray, "Thy Kingdom come, Thy will be done, on earth as it is in heaven."

Rauschenbusch was not only a theologian and a heroic prophet, but he was also a pastor who put into action in New York City his convictions about the social dimensions of the gospel. Serving a church in a section of Manhattan known as "Hell's Kitchen," he saw the consequences of a socioeconomic system structured to serve the interests of the rich while ignoring the disastrous consequences of such favoritism for the poor and politically disinherited. The ugliness of an economic system that offered no decent-paying jobs for desperate parents with hungry children was part of his everyday life. He was a witness to the truth that sin is not simply an expression of an unconverted heart, but also can be the consequence of institutional arrangements that make exploitation of the powerless an inherent necessity. He challenged the church not to simply pacify a discontented populace with promises of pie-in-the-sky-when-they-die, but also to be engaged in the mission of ameliorating the course of history so that the institutions of the societal system might incarnate and express the values taught by Christ.

As an evangelical preacher, I have tried to imitate Rauschenbusch and to communicate to those who will listen that the acceptance of Jesus as Savior is a concomitant to becoming an agent for social change. I have embraced his belief that evangelism is a declaration of the good news of what Christ is doing to transform the world and an invitation to join him in this daring crusade.

Billy Graham is the third giant of Christianity I will cite. He makes me proud to be a Baptist. Not only is he one of my Baptist heroes, but also he stands among the most respected leaders of our generation. Over the years this one-time sectarian tent preacher has grown in stature and in breadth of vision to the point where he represents an ecumenical expression of the best in mass evangelism. Literally millions have responded to his sermons by walking the aisles of auditoriums and outdoor stadiums to declare allegiance to Christ. Billy Graham is regarded around the world as an example of the scandal-free evangelist, while some of his calling have fallen prey to sexual temptation and financial corruption. It is especially heartening that at a time when many mass evangelists have drifted into right-wing politics, Graham has remained nonpartisan, even while taking bold political stands against racism and nuclear arms. Neither Republicans nor Democrats can claim him as a representative of their party, yet both political parties find in him a sense of the spiritual with which each party tries to identify.

Anyone who has ever attended one of Graham's crusade meetings is well aware that something mystical happens when he preaches. What makes this man unique is hard to nail down. The content of his sermons is quite ordinary, and few preachers bother to "steal" his material or quote from the messages he thunders from the pulpit. And while his delivery is powerful and commands rapt attention, there are others whose preaching style generally matches his. What is unmatched when Graham preaches is the presence of the Holy Spirit that seems to fill the air. There is a sense that when he declares the gospel, it is not just an ordinary man in the pulpit, but a special messenger of God. A unique dynamism flows through Billy Graham and generates what sociologist Emile Durkheim might have called "a collective effervescence." All who have witnessed one of Billy Graham's meetings know that this obvious movement of the Holy Spirit is more responsible for the startling responses to his preaching than anything he says or his manner of saying it.

Among those of us who live at the turn of the century, Billy Graham is generally acknowledged as the greatest living Baptist leader. Even those who talk about a "successor" know that his equal is not likely to emerge in this generation. Even so, Graham himself probably would ask, "Who would have expected me to have the opportunity to touch the lives of so many with what the Bible says about Jesus?"

The list of great Baptists is lengthy and would have to include Martin Luther King, Jr., this century's greatest prophet for racial reconciliation and one of the noblest martyrs for the poor, along with primary evangelical theologians such as Carl Henry and progressive theologians such as Harvey Cox and Cornell West. Two of the most articulate preachers of our time, James Forbes of Riverside Church and Peter Gomes of Harvard's Memorial Chapel, are Baptists, too.

Seeing then that we are encompassed with so great a cloud of Baptist witnesses to Christ and to what he is doing in our world, is it any wonder that I want to be a part of this tradition, and that I am proud to share their denominational label? Baptists are fortunate to have many worthy heroes who deserve the allegiance of Christians everywhere.

Building on a Common Faith

———— *Jimmy Carter* ————

Despite our differences, and after almost twenty years of internecine warfare, it is time for all Baptists to put an end to the animosities and bitter words that have separated us as brothers and sisters in Christ.

I was President of the United States in 1979 when the more conservative Southern Baptists gained control of our convention. I was preoccupied with other matters at the time, but somewhat concerned about what was happening. I never dreamed that the hostility would be so deep or long lasting.

As a Southern Baptist and a deacon at Maranatha Baptist Church in Plains, Georgia, I continue to teach Sunday School each week when I'm home, usually to several hundred visitors—only about one-fifth of whom are Baptists. I use outlines and lessons from Baptist literature and quote my father, who was also a deacon and a Sunday School teacher.

I express my own views quite frankly to this mixed audience, not only on the interpretation of biblical texts but also on controversial issues of public interest. I have come to realize much more clearly how different are some of the opinions or beliefs of the people who come to worship together in our small church, but how easy it is for us to agree on the basic principles of our Christian faith. Knowing that many of the visitors are not regular church members and perhaps have never accepted Christ as Savior, I try to insert the plan of salvation into my lesson whenever possible.

It is unlikely that the other members of my church would agree completely with me on all issues, some of which are very controversial.

I believe in the separation of church and state, full autonomy for local congregations, the servanthood of pastors, and full equality of women in Christian service. I know that God made the universe, but not in just six days as we know them, and cannot see where there is any possible conflict between scientific fact and my faith in an omnipotent creator. It is not possible for me to believe that Jesus Christ would approve of either the death penalty or abortion (except perhaps to save the life of a mother). It seems illogical to single out homosexuals for special condemnation, which Jesus never did. In fact, I feel that he wants us to follow him in forgiving others and in realizing that we are all sinners and are not to be judgmental. I know that we are saved by grace through faith in Christ, but try to remember the apostle Paul's words that it is not beneficial to have faith without love.

These brief statements are made to indicate that I, as a Southern Baptist Christian, differ on some issues with most of the people who will read these paragraphs. It would be difficult, if not impossible, for me to change the way I feel just because some pastor, theologian, or a majority of a convention told me I was mistaken. Not being absolutely certain that my beliefs are the only correct ones, I seek guidance through study and prayer. That feeling of being free to do so is what makes me Baptist.

As a prominent layman and a former active leader in the Southern Baptist Convention, I have felt an obligation to seek some accommodation among my fellow Baptists. At the Carter Center during the winter of 1997–1998 Baptist leaders—black, white, Hispanic, liberal, moderate, conservative—met and discussed at great length our differences and compatibilities. We didn't avoid any controversial issues but refrained from making any negative comments about any person. Our unofficial guiding scripture was Ephesians 4:32 (KJV): "And be ye kind one to another, tenderhearted, forgiving one another, even as God for Christ's sake hath forgiven you."

The participants included eight former presidents of the Southern Baptist Convention, several deans and presidents of major Baptist universities, and leaders of other Baptist denominations. With considerable discussion but without any personal animosity, we agreed on a final statement, pledging ourselves to promote a spiritual awakening, to pray for one another, and to treat each other with mutual respect as brothers and sisters in Christ. We also decided to call on all Baptists to work together to eliminate any vestiges of racial discrimination to combat worldwide persecution of Christians. In closing, we pledged "to seek other ways to cooperate to achieve common goals, without breaching our Baptist polity or theological integrity, in order that people may come to know Christ as Savior, and so that God may be glorified in ever increasing measure."

This was a modest beginning, but significant because the participants were some of the most influential Baptists in our nation and found common ground on which to share our faith without rancor. At the same time we recognized that this is not a perfect world, and some of the resentments and misunderstandings are too personal and deep-seated to be erased easily.

We should continue to seek and pray for unity, but it is encouraging to look at the history of our Christian church and to realize that deep divisions, even in the days of the apostles, have often resulted in more enthusiasm and beneficial competition. The fact is that pre-1979 unity in the Southern Baptist Convention is not going to return, but through concerted prayer and an emphasis on the unchanging aspects of our faith, we will be able to move forward even under present difficult circumstances.

From an examination of news reports, it seems that the damage is already being healed among Baptists in America. Last year saw mission giving and baptisms set new records, more students being trained for ministry, more new Baptist churches being formed, and overall giving at a high level.

We Baptists will just have to live with separate efforts being made by the Southern Baptist Convention, the Cooperative Baptist Fellowship, divided state organizations in Texas and Virginia, and individual churches being isolated because of the local congregations' departures from more orthodox tenets of the majority.

God's kingdom is great enough for all of us, and our shared faith in Jesus Christ as our Savior is an adequate foundation for us to live and build together.

Always a Baptist

———— Carolyn Weatherford Crumpler ————

Carolyn W. Crumpler

The gravestones were old and weathered. Moss and ivy were intertwined around the stones, and the big old oak trees hung respectfully over the graveyard. Daddy walked slowly from grave to grave, stopping often to relate an anecdote about the person buried there. Many times I had walked with my father through the cemetery at Pine Grove Baptist Church, but this was my first visit to this one, not far from Pine Grove. This was a special moment, stamped indelibly upon my heart, for I was about to hear a chapter from my family history, my Baptist roots, that I had not heard before. As we stood under the huge old oak trees, looking across the ivy-covered stones, I asked, "Why are there no Weatherfords, or Sansings, or Moores buried here? Why are our kinfolk buried at Pine Grove, or at County Line?"

Daddy stood up straight and pointed his finger at me to give emphasis to what I was about to hear. "Back at the turn of the century some folks came to Pine Grove. They were antimissionary. They said we shouldn't listen to the folks in Jackson (where Mississippi Baptists were based), and they preached all kinds of strange things. Some folks believed them, and they started this church. My family, your mother's family, they all stayed with Baptists, with Southern Baptists."

Now I know! I am a Baptist because generations back my family decided they were Southern Baptists. My answer to "Why am I a Baptist?" begins there. I am a Baptist because I grew up as a Southern Baptist.

We were a church family, and church for us was a white frame building on the south side of Frostproof, Florida. We were a "four-star" church, with Sunday School, BTU (Baptist Training Union), WMU

(Woman's Missionary Union), and a choir. Sometimes we had a Brotherhood organization, but most often not. We had a mixture of pastors, most of them not seminary trained until I was in high school, but all of them were good preachers, strong pastors, and role models for their members. Our worship services were in the traditional revivalist style, and we had two-week revivals every year. We participated in the Orange Blossom Baptist Association, and once in a while our pastor and another leader or two would attend the Florida Baptist Convention meetings. We did our "annual church letter," and we baptized, by immersion, in Clinch Lake, on the west side of Frostproof. We gave through the Cooperative Program, and we always observed the special missions offerings.

I am a Baptist because I am a "church woman." My life in my little hometown was centered in First Baptist Church. That church provided a secure spot where I was loved, nurtured, and discipled. The church family was a family indeed, and we shared our joys and sorrows.

There were three other churches in my hometown—First Methodist, First Presbyterian, and the Church of God. Occasionally the four churches did things together such as a joint Thanksgiving services, a Fourth of July event, or summer revivals under a tent. But my home church was always First Baptist Church, and I never considered becoming a part of one of the other churches.

I was a Baptist, but it was not until my adulthood that I learned there were many different kinds of Baptist. Baptist for me was defined by the Florida Baptist Convention, with offices in Jacksonville. As a girl in GAs (Girls' Auxiliary, WMU's organization for girls 9-16 at the time), I learned about basic Southern Baptist organization. I learned the names of the four boards that "serviced" Southern Baptists—the Foreign Mission Board, the Home Mission Board, the Relief and Annuity Board, and the Sunday School Board. I knew their addresses and the names of the men who headed them. I learned about the Cooperative Program, which was birthed five years before I came into the world. I could "divide the pie," knowing how much money stayed in my church, how much stayed in Florida, and how the rest was divided when it got to Nashville, Tennessee. I was a Baptist because of the education programs and the organization of the Southern Baptist Convention.

When I was sixteen years old, a friend and I rode the Greyhound bus to Jacksonville, where we joined a busload of high school and college girls from across the state for YWA (Young Woman's Auxiliary) Week at Ridgecrest Baptist Assembly in North Carolina. I saw my first mountain! I met those four men who headed the four boards, and I was very much impressed that those great leaders were willing to come to speak to us. I met missionaries. The work that had begun in my own little church was brought to fruition there in the mountains. I knew that God had a special place of service for me, and that it would be as a Baptist, called into "full-time Christian service," as we said in those days.

Back in Frostproof I told my parents what I had decided. I talked to my pastor, who told me that if God was calling me to special service, I had to begin to serve him where I was. I was already a Sunday School teacher for nine- and ten-year-old boys. Then I became Vacation Bible School principal for the first VBS to be held at First Baptist Church. Helping us to get it started was our "field secretary," who was responsible for the southwest portion of Florida—quite a field for B. D. Locke! With guidance from my pastor, my parents, and the field secretary, I was on my way to being trained. That was 1946, and there was never a thought that a call to a sixteen-year-old girl would be to the ministry.

During my senior year in high school, in addition to teaching the boys' Sunday School class, I became the choir leader. We had a "singing school" after Vacation Bible School, and the lady from Jacksonville who led the school decided that I could lead the singing better than any of the other folks. My music career lasted only that one year!

Going to Florida State University opened a new Southern Baptist avenue for me—the BSU (Baptist Student Union). Situated adjacent to the big campus was a red brick building, placed there by the Florida Baptist Convention and staffed by a woman employed as student secretary. BSU helped me to transfer my First Baptist Frostproof persona to First Baptist, then Lakeview Baptist, Tallahassee. Again, pastors and lay leaders nurtured me, opened doors for me, and loved me. After graduating from college and becoming a school teacher, I continued my Baptist education, and my growing Baptist identity. I became a "state-approved worker" and led conferences on stewardship, missions education, and young adult Sunday School. I served as associational Training Union leader, and through those experiences became a devoted Southern Baptist organization person. We really had an excellent system of leadership training, fellowship, and world vision.

As a young adult, then, I was a Baptist because of the local church life and fellowship, the excellent structure of support and training, he services provided by state and national offices, and the vision for world missions. In the summers I worked in mission camps, directed Vacation Bible Schools, and just enjoyed being a Baptist.

As my friendship circle expanded beyond home, church, and school, I discovered another reason for being Baptist. Friends of other persuasions seemed to be bound to certain beliefs, practices, rules, and regulations. I began to understand the principle of freedom, and New Testament teachings about the freedom provided by Christ, and the warnings against being in bondage again after being freed by Christ. When friends would bring out their catechism, book of principles, or whatever, I realized that I did not have a book to follow except the Bible. I began to study the Bible as my source of belief and practice. I became a free Baptist. Even before I learned that this was a priceless Baptist freedom, I claimed it for myself.

It was in a traditional Baptist revival service that I renewed my early commitment to a church-related vocation. As the evangelist, a professor of Bible in a Baptist university, concluded his sermon one evening, he quoted this prayer: "Lord, send me anywhere, only go with me; place any burden on me, only sustain me; sever any tie, save the tie that binds my heart to yours." God spoke to my heart through that prayer, and as we sang the "Baptist invitation"—"Just As I Am"—I walked to the front of the church and committed myself to seminary and then missions or whatever.

Years later I had the opportunity to share that experience with Dr. Charles Howard, the evangelist. His response was, "Carolyn, I remember that revival as my all-time failure. No response. Dead. Thank you for telling me that it was not a failure!"

Then the decision about seminary had to be made. Most of the people I knew who had been to seminary had attended the Southern Baptist Theological Seminary in Louisville, Kentucky. I didn't want to

go to Southern, but I didn't know why. After hearing a home missionary from New Orleans, Gladys Keith, speak at a missions meeting, I
decided that New Orleans Seminary was for me. Seminole Heights
Baptist Church, my adult home church, endorsed me, and I left for
New Orleans. Dr. Roland Q. Leavell was the president, Dr. Frank Stagg
was my New Testament professor, Dr. Penrose St. Amant was my
church history professor, and Dr. Helen Falls taught missions education and later all the missions courses in the School of Theology. What
a way to learn Baptist!

That was 1956, and I learned something I had never thought of. I
had to enroll in the School of Religious Education because I was
female. I was not musical (in spite of my choral directing!), so that left
only religious education. It was not until several years after I graduated
that the first woman would enroll in theology. Even so, my seminary
experience was a very satisfying, growing experience. I began to learn
that I was indeed a Baptist, and that there were many deep, significant
reasons for that. Even today I stand in awe of the people whose lives
converged with mine in the city of New Orleans.

Two other Baptist spots in New Orleans contributed to those rich
and wonderful days. I joined First Baptist Church, where Dr. J. D. Grey
was my pastor. I also worked full-time at Mather School of Nursing at
Southern Baptist Hospital. Miss Mather was still there as director, and
between Dr. Grey and Miss Mather I received profound extracurricular
training.

After graduating from New Orleans Baptist Theological Seminary,
I spent thirty-one years working with Woman's Missionary Union. I
served twice on the staff of Alabama WMU, and twice on the Florida
staff. Then for fifteen years I served as the fifth executive director of
Woman's Missionary Union. During that time I had the privilege of
leading in the celebration of the centennial of WMU, the only auxiliary
of the Southern Baptist Convention.

Beginning with New Orleans Seminary, and continuing through
my years with Woman's Missionary Union, I came to understand and
to accept with my total being the principles of being Baptist. Working
in two states, appreciating the separateness of the church, association,
state, and national entities, yet recognizing the togetherness, I knew the

soundness of our kind of convention organization. Relating to Baptists of other stripes, I came to a stronger commitment to Southern Baptists and our ways of getting the job done.

I must repeat that I am a Baptist because I was a Southern Baptist. That firm rock began to erode, however. As controversy began to consume our lives, I strongly avowed: "This isn't about WMU. We will stick to our job, which is missions." As I came to admit that the struggle was about everything I had worked for, I had to admit that the Southern Baptist Convention to which I had committed myself was no longer there.

Meanwhile, I had married and moved away from the center of activity. I joined the church where my husband was pastor for thirty years before he retired in 1992. Founded in 1822, and becoming Southern Baptist in the mid-1950s, Mt. Carmel Baptist Church would become my current safety net. That began to change, however, and I was faced with the big question: "Am I really a Baptist? Can I not become Methodist, or Presbyterian, or something else? After all, aren't we all alike, basically?" So I began to look, and to ponder, and to pray, and to wish for an easy answer. The answer was an easy one, after all: "I am a Baptist. I want to stay a Baptist. I will be a Baptist in a Baptist church."

Why am I a Baptist? Let me to give you some reasons:

• I am a Baptist because I am free in Christ to follow him, to learn of him.

• I am a Baptist because God has given me His holy Word and the Holy Spirit to interpret for me the meaning and application of that Word.

• I am a Baptist because I believe that Christ established the church and that God works through the church to accomplish His will and purpose today.

• I am a Baptist because I believe that the work of the church is separate from the work of the government, that my responsibility to each can be carried out with a clear separation of the roles of the two, and that as a Christian I can exercise my responsible citizenship in both.

• I am a Baptist because my local expression of the church is found in a local congregation that is free under the leadership of the Spirit to do the work of the Kingdom, without direction or coercion from another source.

• I am a Baptist because I believe that we accept the challenge of Christ's commission to "go into all the world," which we can do without a hierarchy.

• I am a Baptist because I like our understanding of worship, its place, and its necessity.

Now, how can I be a Baptist without being a Southern Baptist? That is a difficult question, but it is not unanswerable. Although through the powerful channel of home and foreign missions Southern Baptists were about to get into all the world, they are not the only ones out there. It is important to me that we go, and I believe we can do it.

Claiming Your Inheritance
— James C. Denison —

There is an old Indian fable about a brave who was walking through the forest one day and found an eagle's egg. He picked it up and took it home, but soon realized that he had no idea what to do with such a thing. And so he set the egg in a nest of prairie chickens. In due time the egg hatched, and the eagle was born. He looked around himself and saw only prairie chickens, so the eagle assumed he was a prairie chicken, too.

The eagle learned to do what prairie chickens do. He scratched around in the dirt for food and flew by flapping his wings in a fluttering of feathers just a few feet off the ground. Years went by, and the eagle grew old.

Then one day the eagle heard a shriek high overhead. He looked up into a brilliantly blue, cloudless sky and saw a magnificent creature. Golden wings barely moved as it floated high up in the heavens. He turned to the prairie chicken at his side and said, "What is that?" The prairie chicken said, "Oh, that's an eagle. But don't give it a second thought—you could never be like him." And so he never gave it a second thought, and the eagle spent the rest of his life as a prairie chicken, because he didn't know who he was.

The fable makes this point: you may not be able to choose *where* you are, but you can always choose *who* you are. Often you cannot control your circumstances. Elections are won and lost, power gained and controlled. But no one can take from you the right to determine your own identity. You can still choose who you are.

My purpose here is to encourage us to be who we are. We are Baptists. First, a brief word regarding my own background.

I was born and raised in Houston, Texas, where I went to high school and college. My father had been a Methodist Sunday school teacher before he enlisted in the army during World War II, but following the atrocities he saw in the war, he didn't go to church much.

We didn't go to church much as a family either. Our family was strong and supportive, with a deep commitment to morality and character, but church just wasn't a part of our lifestyle. I considered myself a Christian because I tried to be a good person and I believed in God. That's how most Americans define "Christian," and that's what I thought.

When I was fifteen, everything changed. College Park Baptist Church started a bus ministry, knocking on doors and inviting people in the area to ride the bus to church. One Saturday in August 1973, Julian Unger and Tony McGrady knocked on my apartment door and invited me and my younger brother to their church. We didn't want to go, but Dad thought we should, so he put us on the bus the next day.

I'll never forget that first Sunday. I didn't know Job from John. I brought our big family Bible to church and wore my only tie and "church" shoes. They sang, "There is a Balm in Gilead," but I didn't know what a balm was or where Gilead was. I didn't understand the sermon or the Sunday school lesson. The whole day was a bad experience, and I wasn't interested in repeating it.

But the church members wouldn't give up. They kept visiting us, praying for us, and inviting us. So we kept riding their bus to church. I became impressed with their love for each other, a kind of joy I'd never seen before. I wanted it for myself. Finally, on September 9, 1973, I asked my Sunday school teacher how I could have what they had, and she led me to personal faith in Jesus Christ. Six months later my brother became a believer. A year or so afterward we were baptized together. Mark is now the pastor of a church in Houston he planted some ten years ago. We'll always be grateful for that church bus.

And so I became a Christian as a result of the outreach of a Southern Baptist church, and all I've ever been my entire Christian life is a Southern Baptist. From high school and the youth group of my church I went to Houston Baptist University on a scholarship provided by Texas Baptists. During college I worked on the staff of two Southern

Baptist churches and preached in dozens more. I served overseas as a Southern Baptist summer missionary.

After college I married, and Janet and I moved to Southwestern Baptist Theological Seminary. I became the pastor of a Southern Baptist church and eventually served Southwestern as a faculty member in the philosophy of religion. For those years I was literally an employee of the Southern Baptist Convention. From Southwestern I moved to the pastorate of First Baptist Church in Midland, Texas, the leading church in Cooperative Program giving in Texas across the last quarter-century. From Midland I went to Second-Ponce de Leon Baptist Church in Atlanta, Georgia, one of the leading Cooperative Program churches in that state. Today I am privileged to serve as pastor of Park Cities Baptist Church in Dallas, Texas. In other words, I've been a Southern Baptist.

But I haven't been just any Southern Baptist. I'm the product of very conservative Southern Baptists. My home church would have been considered "fundamentalist" today. I heard Paige Patterson preach several times. My first study Bible was a Scofield Reference Bible, and my first biblical commentary was written by Hal Lindsey. My roots are in the soil of conservative Southern Baptist life.

Across the years I came to learn what Baptists are, what we believe, what we stand for. The more I learned, the more grateful I became. From then to today, I am proud to be a Baptist. I believe that Baptist theology preserves some of the vital distinctives of New Testament faith. I am convinced that Baptist polity and doctrine are essential to the vitality of the church today. I became a believer as a Baptist, and I am proud that I'm still a Baptist.

Here's the problem: Apparently many Baptists no longer believe what I was told Baptists believe. I haven't changed, but the Southern Baptist Convention has. I still embrace the basic distinctives of Baptist faith and practice, but many of those leading the Southern Baptist Convention today no longer do. I haven't left them; they've left me. Let me explain.

"No Creed but the Bible"

The first Baptist doctrine I was taught is simple: "Baptists have no creed but the Bible." I was told that Baptists first came into being because they opposed the creeds their churches were forcing them to sign. They refused to force one man's doctrine on another. They had no statement I must sign, no particular way of stating their faith that I must follow. I was told that all Scripture is inspired by God, and that's good enough for Baptists.

Tragically, this is no longer true. "Inerrancy" is now the means by which SBC leaders measure your theology and mine. This is uncharted territory for Baptists. Never before have we developed one doctrinal formulation and required it of each other. Those leading the SBC have taken us where we've never been before.

My doctoral dissertation was in biblical hermeneutics; I also taught this subject at Southwestern Seminary. I have therefore become familiar with the doctrine of "inerrancy." I have discovered eight major definitions of the term itself, all held by "conservative" scholars. I also have found at least twelve major qualifications of the term.[1] If you call yourself an "inerrantist," I must ask you which definition you mean and which qualifications you accept. As a result, the word has no practical, clear meaning today.

In addition, "inerrancy" applies only to the original biblical manuscripts, none of which we possess today. Now the Chicago Statement on Biblical Inerrancy, the standard to which most "inerrantists" subscribe, admits that the biblical copies we do possess "are not entirely error-free" (Exposition, section E). And yet "inerrancy" is necessary to preserve the trustworthiness of the text. We therefore have this logical puzzle: (1) The text must be inerrant to be trustworthy. (2) The copies we possess today "are not entirely error-free." (3) Therefore, they are by definition not trustworthy. The argument thus minimizes the only Bible we do have and defeats its very purpose. For good reason, Baptists have avoided creeds.

I am a Baptist because I believe what Baptists have historically said: No creed but the Bible. You can say it's right or it's wrong to have a creed, but you cannot say it's Baptist. I choose to be Baptist.

Servant Leadership

Second, I was taught that Baptists believe in servant leadership. In this we follow the example of Jesus himself.

In John 13 Jesus did something no Jew could be made to do, not even a Jewish slave. He wrapped himself in a towel and took a wash basin. Then, on his hands and knees, he washed the dirty, mud-caked feet of his disciples. He washed the feet of Peter, who would deny him, and of Judas, who would betray him. He told us to do likewise.

I was told that Baptists seek to fulfill Christ's command in their model of leadership. Unlike many other denominations, Baptists insist that their leaders be servants. We have no "hierarchy," which means literally "the rule of priests." We have no denominational or ecclesiastical control of our churches and people. Our pastors love their people and serve them. This is the Baptist way.

But things have changed. Now many of our leaders say the pastor is the "ruler" of the church. I know some who call themselves "benevolent dictators." We're told that the way to grow a church is to control it. We are now hearing and seeing an entire model of leadership that is anything but servanthood.

You can say this is right, or you can say it's wrong, but you cannot say it's Baptist. I choose to be Baptist.

The Priesthood of Every Christian

Third, I was taught that Baptists believe in the "priesthood" of every Christian. According to 1 Peter 2:9, we are a "royal priesthood." Baptists from the beginning have taken this concept literally. We have always taught that each person is responsible for his or her personal relationship with God, that he or she should be baptized only after such a personal commitment to Jesus Christ, and that he or she is then free to interpret and apply the faith personally. Baptists have historically stood for the principle that each of us is equal before God and has the privilege and responsibility to interpret the Bible for ourselves.

Again, things have changed. A few years ago at a national Southern Baptist conference I heard one of our leading pastors say, "I am the sole arbiter of theology for my church." I've been to other conferences where I've heard the same idea expressed. The pastor interprets the text for the people—his word is God's word—and to disagree with him is to disagree with the word of God on the subject.

You can say this is right, or you can say it's wrong, but you cannot say it's Baptist. I choose to be Baptist.

A Free Church in a Free State

Last, I was taught that Baptists believe in a free church in a free state. When Jesus declared, "Give to Caesar what is Caesar's, and to God what is God's" (Matt 22:21), he settled this issue. Baptists have historically stood on his words.

Baptists believe in a free state. In studying Baptist history I learned that the first people to formulate the doctrine of the separation of church and state in the English language were John Smyth and Thomas Helwys, the first leaders of the Baptist movement. I discovered that many Baptists over the centuries had died for this principle.

Now things are different. I've heard leaders in the SBC declare that the separation of church and state is a myth; some say they're "out to rewrite the First Amendment." One said on national television, "I believe this notion of the separation of church and state was the figment of some infidel's imagination." That's not Baptist.

Baptists also believe in a free church. We have stood for autonomous local churches with no political control from any outside group. We send "messengers" to our conventions, not "delegates," and they are to vote their free wills and consciences. Their votes have no binding authority on their churches. And no political group can have control of our denomination or churches.

But things are different today. Some say that the group controlling the SBC has sought theological "correction" and used political means only because they are necessary. Others say that this group has sought political control and used theological issues only because they are necessary. Which is true?

Here's one answer. In May 1986 Dr. James L. Sullivan, retired president of the Sunday School Board, spoke to employees on "Anniversary Day." Here are some of his remarks:

I came across this denominational problem in 1970. That was nine years before it surfaced and became public. I discovered that a man whom I knew quite well in a state on the Eastern Seaboard was an associate editor of a magazine publishing things that weren't precisely true. I called him and asked for a conference and spent several hours in his presence to try and pick his mind and see how he was thinking. Among other things, he said, "We're going to do whatever it takes to take over the state conventions and the Southern Baptist Convention, and we intend to do it as quickly as it can be accomplished."

First, he stated that he was mad with the system by which trustees were elected, not at us as an institution. But he attacked the institution to get at the trustees.

The second thing was his determination to control both state conventions and the Southern Baptist Convention, and he was not secretive or apologetic about it. The third thing was that he identified some of the leaders by name. To show how well they have succeeded, he named four men to me. One became a parliamentarian almost immediately, and three others are now serving as trustees on Southern Baptist boards and agencies in fulfillment of his stated determination. I asked him how he was going to accomplish his purpose, and he said, "We're going to organize the losers of every election and cause of Southern Baptist history we can identify."

He said, "Winners soon forget, but losers never do. The South is still fighting the Civil War. The North forgot there ever was one." He felt if they could identify and organize the losers, they would have the majority.

Next, I said, "Under what special issue are you going to fly a flag?" He said, "We haven't picked it yet, but when we pick it, it will be one that no one can give rebuttal to without hopelessly getting himself into controversy." . . . That's the background under which the controversy started seven years before it openly surfaced.[2]

Those leaders chose their theological issue well, but political control was their purpose. I have spoken to some of their leaders personally and heard them say that their goal is to control the state conventions and the local churches as they have the Southern Baptist Convention. A "free church" is no longer their concern.

You can say this is right, or you can say it's wrong, but you cannot say it's Baptist. I choose to be Baptist.

✝✝✝✝

Today we want to be defined by what we are, not by what we are not. We do not want to be defined by what we oppose, but by what we affirm. So let us affirm what we believe and who we are. Let us embrace our identity. We are Baptists.

And because we are Baptists, we still believe in no creed but the Bible. We still believe in servant leadership. We still believe in the priesthood of every Christian. We still believe in a free church in a free state.

These beliefs matter. They are the critical foundation for relevant mission and ministry today. We can best "make disciples of all nations" (Matt 28:19) when we preach only the Bible, when we serve and love people, when we empower and equip every Christian for discipleship and ministry, and when we serve no authority but Jesus Christ. If we depart from these principles, we leave the church of the New Testament, and we stop being Baptist. Let's be Baptists.

I will close with a story from my favorite preacher, Dr. Fred Craddock. Dr. Craddock is professor emeritus of New Testament and preaching at Candler School of Theology, Emory University, in Atlanta, Georgia. He is also one of the finest storytellers of this generation.

One of my favorite Craddock stories comes from a time when Dr. Craddock and his wife were on vacation a number of years ago in Gatlinburg, Tennessee, in the Smoky Mountains. They stopped for dinner at one of their favorite restaurants, the Black Bear Inn. It was a beautiful place to eat, with plate glass windows across one entire wall so you could look over the hills and mountains and enjoy the scenery.

As Dr. Craddock tells the story, he and his wife are at their table crawling through this fancy menu looking for hamburgers when an elderly gentleman stops by. A big shock of gray hair. He says, "Good evening." Dr. Craddock says, "Good evening." The man says, "Are you on vacation?" Fred says, "Well, yes." "Where are you from?" "We're from Atlanta." "What do you do back in Atlanta?" Well, that was no business of his, but Fred thinks he might be the proprietor, and so he says, "I work at a seminary. I teach preachers." The elderly gentleman says, "You teach preachers? I've got a story about a preacher." And he pulls out a chair and sits down right at their table.

Now this is just what you want on your vacation—another preacher story. The gentleman begins, "I was born back here in these hills. My mother wasn't married. And the reproach that fell on her fell on me. The other kids had a name for me, and it hurt, a lot. I would go into town, and everyone would stop and stare. I knew they were trying to figure out who my father was. It was a very hard time.

"About that time the church down the street got a new preacher, and he fascinated me and scared me at the same time. He had a big stone jaw and wore a top hat and tailcoat and had a voice that thundered. I'd come each Sunday to listen to him preach, but I didn't want anyone to see me in church and say, 'What's a boy like you doing in our church?' So I'd wait until the service had started, and then I'd slip in the back door and into the back pew. As soon as he finished the last word of his sermon, I would jump up and run out before anyone could see me or stop me.

"This went on for weeks. One day I don't know what happened, but by the time I got up, it was too late. People were already in the aisles, standing in the door, and the way was blocked. I was trapped, and I couldn't get out. I was nervous and sweating, and I just knew that someone was going to see me and say, 'What's a boy like you doing in here?'

"Just then I felt a hand on my shoulder. I turned and looked, and there was that top hat and that stone jaw. The preacher, with his voice of thunder. With a stern look on his face, he pointed his finger at me and said, 'Boy, I know who your daddy is.'

"My heart sank. It was the worst moment of my life. That preacher pointed his finger at me and said, 'Boy, you're a child of . . . You're a child of . . .' Then he smiled real big and said, 'Son, you're a child of the King.' He swatted me on the rear and then said, 'Go, claim your inheritance.'"

Dr. Craddock looked at the elderly gentleman and said, "Sir, what's your name?" "Ben Hooper," he replied. Then Fred remembered his father telling him about the time when for two terms the people of Tennessee elected an illegitimate governor named Ben Hooper.

The word for us is: Baptists, claim your inheritance. Embrace what you believe and who you are. We're children of the King.

Notes

[1]See my article, "Inerrancy: Definitions and Qualifications," newsletter, *Texas Baptists Committed* (July 1994) 9.

[2]"James L. Sullivan addresses question of SBC turbulence," *Facts and Trends* (July-August 1986) 10-11.

Yes, I Am a Baptist

——— *James M. Dunn* ———

"**M**iz Lillian," President Carter's mother, grudgingly but cordially met a reporter at the door of her Plains, Georgia, home. Jimmy was running for President, telling Americans, "I'll never lie to you." The reporter, some sort of Yankee, tested the senior sister Carter's patience. "Hasn't Jimmy Carter ever lied?" he asked. "Oh, maybe, little white lies," mother Carter responded. "What is a white lie?" he pushed. "Oh, you know," she said, "like the one I told when I greeted you just now: 'It's so good to see you.'"

I was "brung up" with that standard for honesty. In our home a smile was sincere, a scowl was a scold, and a compliment was a gracious gift. Admonitions, which I'm sure with Dr. Spocks were far too frequent, and every single rebuff were honest attempt to help me and my sister, Ann, learn to make good choices on our own. We understood that, even then. Hard-core honesty lavered with love left no doubt in our minds about where our parents stood or who they were or that we were loved.

To this good day I have trouble saying "It's so good to see you" when it's not. Small talk with mean-spirited people is difficult. I've thought a lot about that.

Oh, I know, it was indeed a certain lack of socialization on the part of my parents, both children of sharecroppers. But it was much more than slim sophistication. Mother and Daddy had no patience with pretension. They could not stand people "putting on."

The other side of that coin of tough truthfulness, lived as well as said, was immense respect for every last person with whom they came in contact. They "loved folks just because they are folks," as T. B. Maston used to say.

In retrospect I've finally seen it. There is a two-sidedness to high expectation for candid, apparent, what-you-see-is-what-you-get personality on one hand and remarkable respect for every individual on the other. If people are what they present themselves to be, what more can one ask?

My parents came by these virtues honestly. Their little frame Baptist church at Cottonwood, Kaufman County, was the locus of a fellowship that was formative. They took scripture seriously—boy, did they! Spiritual formation suffused every ordinary chore. Hymn singing accompanied daily duties.

They had a primal insight into every human being as one made in God's image and one for whom Christ died. That permanent perspective instilled infinite respect for persons. That understanding of humanity included the view that one makes his own choices and lives with them. We are becoming more like ourselves every day by the slow stain of choice.

Whatever else the doctrine of *imago dei* involves, it means that we can respond to God. And much of our trouble and pain we bring upon ourselves. On the other hand, "you can do whatever you set your mind to." "Not failure, but low aim is crime." Everyone is able to respond; we are response-able, responsible, and free.

Not a nuanced theology but durable and deep, that elemental understanding that was ours for the acceptance of one's own person-hood. We knew in our innards that all persons were valuable and fallible and free.

Hard honesty kept me from "going down the aisle" at church until I knew I meant it. Our church crept as close to compulsion as it could. The pastor fostered what we later came to call "trap services." Some of the preachers would literally try to scare the hell out of us. I resisted. I knew I was responsible for my own decision. When a kinder, gentler pastor came, I accepted Christ. All that may sound unconnected to why I am a Baptist, but it's not.

Before falling into the clutches of manipulative Baptist evangelists, my family went to East Broadway Presbyterian Church in Fort Worth,

Texas. It was wonderful. Lots of Bible. Pastors who qualified every pon-tification with "as I understand it" or "my own belief is." I can still smell the flour and water paste we made in Vacation Bible School and remember holding high my first pocket watch to signal the preacher that I'd had enough sermon.

Our best neighbors were Campbellites (Church of Christ). So my childhood was about as ecumenical as one could expect on the south side of Fort Worth. Years later when college came I had a heavy dose of Methodism at Texas Wesleyan College. It was the right school for me: small enough to know everyone, caring professors, a healthy atmos-phere of experienced religion.

Through these experiences my religion was forming what I later learned to call "theology." Some of the elemental components were:

• respect for every person who like every pot sits on his or her own bottom, responsible and free

• a presupposition that even God will not violate the faculty given to every human to decide for him/herself

• a belief that God, taking on flesh and blood and temptations like mine, in the human but divine Jesus, cared for me personally and for every other human being on the face of the earth

• a conscientious objection to running roughly over the freedom of any mortal, because they are all shaped like God and dignified to great worth because Jesus took on flesh like ours for our sake

When Ralph Phelps, an ethics professor at Southwestern Baptist Theological Seminary, applied the gospel to race relations, he made me mad. But because of my own upbringing, I saw that he was right.

When Stewart Newman, a philosophy prof, taught one of those tiresome five-night-two-hours-every-night-study courses on what Baptists believe, it rang true. He introduced me to soul freedom, religious liberty, and the separation of church and state.

When years later I was exposed to Senator Ralph Yarborough's political populism and passion for working people, I understood. He, by his own clear testimony, got his political philosophy right out of his Baptist beliefs.

I also understood when John Kenneth Galbraith told David Frost that his "economics for everyman" probably came from teaching at his Baptist mother's knee about the freedom and dignity of persons deemed by God to be worth the blood of Christ.

It was not trickle-down theology from the top but bubble-up belief born of experience that exposed me to Baptists. As Grady Cothen puts it, "transactions with God on our own" were the norm, the self-evident standard for religious experience.

How could anyone possibly believe anything else? Unless religion is free, voluntary, personal, intimate, and inward, it's not worth anything anyway. No. It's worse than worthless, because if it's secondhand, it may well keep one from ever experiencing the real thing, a vital, visceral, life-changing faith.

Our religion is more a matter of relationships, human and divine, than rational exercise, and our theology, rightly "incarnational," is essentially a relationship with Jesus Christ. Theology, then, interprets religion, rather than religion merely expressing theology. Some of us identify with E. Y. Mullins' approach to our faith. In *The Christian Religion in Its Doctrinal Expression* he had no patience with theology as a "system of philosophy" or "abstract intellectualism."

Absolutely no coercion can exist in matters of faith. The coercive state has no business messing with religion. When government touches religion, it always has the touch of mud. When anyone's religious freedom is denied, everyone's religious freedom is endangered.

On the thinking level, then, my sticking with Baptists is related to the experiential emphasis. The "I" at the center of our being even Almighty God will not trample. George W. Truett spoke to this Baptist doggedness in his famous sermon on the steps of the United States Capitol:

> The right to private judgment is the crown jewel of humanity, and for any person or institution to come between God and the soul is a blasphemous impertinence and a defamation of the crown rights of the Son of God.

So experience, not expectations, even expectations of family or church, makes for authentic Christian faith. Then personal allegiance to a living Lord, not propositions, marks genuine Baptist testimony.

A fundamentalist leader of the Southern Baptist departure from baptistness shared his personal views at a meeting in Nashville, Tennessee. He said, "I learned when I was at Princeton that I cannot believe anything I cannot understand." Poor little fellow. Where is faith? C. S. Lewis said, "If one can believe only what he can understand, he can write his creed on a postage stamp."

We have no binding creed, but we have a freedom that encourages, no, mandates, personal interpretation of Scripture. Our confession of faith is the most ancient, the most accessible, the most biblical, the most universal, the most pregnant with ethical and moral meaning of any Christian confession of faith. It is simply, "Jesus Christ is Lord."

If we have anything remotely resembling a creed, it is the Baptist oral tradition that insists, "Ain't nobody but Jesus going to tell me what to believe."

Finally, it is a relationship to Jesus Christ, not a rational scheme that puts one right with God. Call it too subjective. Call it gnostic. Say that it is cowboy Christianity with "every man's hat his church." Baptists have historically held the objective-subjective balance between *sola scriptura* and *sola fide*. No list of laws, no articles of assent, no head trip makes one righteous. Rather, repentance and faith are steps of grace.

In a wonderful little book, *The Pattern of Authority*, Bernard Ramm suggests that Baptist Christians find their ultimate authority in the living Lord, Jesus Christ as revealed in scripture, or the scripture as it becomes the Living Word through the work of Jesus Christ in our lives. Doesn't matter which way you say it, does it?

Conformity, convention, coercion, and consensus cannot redeem. In fact, "free" and "faithful" are the hallmarks of real Baptists.

On a feeling level I've found the faith mediated to me by Baptists to be worthy. Who hasn't sung, "tempted and tried we're oft made to wonder, why it should be thus all the day long"? Even if you don't know the song, you've felt the feeling. In 1974 invasive melanoma planted me in the Stehlin Research Institute for a month and had me planning my funeral. My faith was tested. I came to know "the peace that passes understanding."

When the experiences of life shake you by the nape of the neck like a mother cat claims back a kitten, faith is tested. When everything you believe is challenged, faith is tested. The vitality of a baptist-kind of religious experience has served me well. Not smaltzy sentimentality. Not polyanna happy face. Not steely stoicism. But faithing my way forward has been sustained in the Baptist fellowship.

Plenty of folks labeled "Baptist" embarrass me—television entrepreneurs, sleazy politicians, cocksure fundamentalists. But Baptists, on our good days, when we are living up to our profession of faith, are a breed with whom I'm proud to claim kinship.

We find evangelism and ministry and mission fueled by love. We find passion for peace and justice and meeting human need. We find the pursuit of truth and learning and art and free expression. We find personal spiritual growth and maturity and Christian insight. Much of what moderns search for they can find if they encounter a better bunch of Baptists. Such families of faith do exist.

However, in Washington when I tell someone "Yes, I'm a Baptist and I work for Baptists," their response often drips with snide. I hurriedly say, "But I'm a Bill Moyers, Jimmy Carter, Barbara Jordan kind of Baptist."

How about you?

Jocelyn the Baptist
A Legacy of Divine Faith

———— Jocelyn L. Foy ————

What John the Baptist is in the realm of spirit-filled servants, what the apostle Peter is in the birth of the Christian church, and what Rosa Parks is as the matriarch of the civil rights movement, so is the Baptist church centered at the very core of my being.

It has been said, "Once Baptist gets in your blood, it is hard to wash out." Baptist blood has flowed through my family's veins for more than one hundred years. The character of these spiritual believers has been instilled in me by my parents and nurtured by my church. Why I choose to worship God in the context of the Baptist tradition and choose to continue honoring such a rich legacy has as much to do with who I am and who I have become as it does to who I hope to become in the new millennium.

For as long as I have embraced the significance of my African ancestry, I have understood that I am an heir of a strong Baptist lineage. I am the product of people of slavery whose divine faith in God sustained them. I have explored their tragedies and triumphs over the years and have grown to appreciate their impact on my life.

Several years ago, as a graduate student at North Carolina A&T State University in the adult education masters degree program, I researched my genealogy and discovered the Baptist cornerstones of both of my parents' families. Primarily for these reasons I am committed to preserving the Baptist heritage. The following spiritual memoir is offered in an effort to address my Baptist witness at the close of this century and the beginning of another.

Perhaps the most notable Baptist patriarch of my family was my paternal great-grandfather, the late Reverend Thornton Hairston, who served as a minister at the turn of this century. His pilgrimage of faith and profound leadership was significant for five generations of Baptist descendants. I am told he was an orator of great character, great civility, great conviction, and great commitment to his God. I often wonder what he must have preached to his congregations, especially regarding the relationship between one's faith and race relations in light of the emancipation of slaves. Whatever his message, it bears repeating today for our generations.

A native of Davie County and one of the very few college-trained Negroes of his time, his vocation as an educator for twenty-five years was interrupted when he "heard the call to preach." According to my paternal grandmother, the late Shulelvia Hairston Foy, my great-grandfather often talked of confrontations in which he engaged with "Marse Frank," the owner of the Cooleemee Plantation.

It seemed that "Marse Frank" was quite displeased with the length of my great-grandfather's Sunday services, as it delayed his dinner preparations. He suggested, therefore, to my great-grandfather that he shorten the services to permit his servants to serve the meal at a time more to his liking. The message was clear. My great-grandfather refused to accommodate him, however. In essence, he informed "Marse Frank" that he should inform the servants of his desire, and if they thought it necessary to excuse themselves from the services, he would make no attempt to hold them further. My great-grandfather politely indicated his belief that servants should be concerned with the wishes of their masters. With regard to the length of the church service, he made it known that he felt he was acting as God's servant and that he would follow God's dictates on the matter, not those of "Marse Frank."

At the time my great-grandfather served as pastor of some four Baptist congregations in the Davie and Davidson County areas— Cedar Grove, The People's Grove, Yadkin Star, and Petersville. He traveled to several of them via "Marse Frank's" ferry. I am told that "Marse Frank" was so infuriated that he denied my great-grandfather the convenience of the ferry, thus requiring him to go on foot several miles to accomplish his journey. This he did for several years.

The happy ending to this story is that after several years, "Marse Frank" found an occasion to visit my great-grandfather to indicate that he had watched him rather carefully and had others to do so to determine if he had trespassed on the land access or ferry that had been denied him. Not once had he done so. Thus, "Marse Frank" had come to state that he found such manly behavior commendable. He also removed the earlier barrier and offered my great-grandfather the use of his land as a peace offering.

In 1902 my great-grandfather was called as the third pastor of Shiloh Baptist Church, which still stands in Winston-Salem, North Carolina. Under his pastorate Shiloh made splendid progress, both spiritually and fiscally. Two sanctuaries were built, and hundreds of souls were won for Christ. He remained there for seventeen years until his death in 1919. It is evident that his understanding of Baptist doctrines included the empowerment of the Holy Spirit to be God's vessel, the authority to serve as God's spokesperson for social justice, the personal interpretation and application of biblical scriptures, the freedom of thought and expression (both in and out of the pulpit), and the lordship of Jesus Christ. These principles served as the catalyst for my great-grandfather's courageous behavior.

My grandmother often spoke of her father with reverence and admiration as if she wanted to be like him. His influence left such an indelible mark on her life that she took 2 Timothy 2:15 literally and "studied to show herself approved unto God." However, sometime during her adulthood, while serving as an organist for several Baptist congregations in Winston-Salem, North Carolina, she, too, "heard the call of God to preach." Although she knew that because of her gender she would be denied the endorsement by Shiloh Baptist Church (the church of her father's pastorate and the place of her conversion) to become licensed to preach, she refused to allow the proposed injustices to muzzle God's gift within her. Hence, her front porch became her pulpit. She preached the gospel with passion to anyone who would dare to listen—whether neighbor or mailman, the local drunk or the local politician. While many heard the Word and were enlightened by the Spirit, few dared to challenge her knowledge of the Scriptures. Needless to say, "Mama Shug" was surely the most devout person I have ever known. And she was most assuredly every bit a woman!

Somehow the faith of this grandmother, which was born in the heart of the Baptist culture, settled in the soul of my father, the late Bernard Thornton Foy, Sr. Similarly, this same faith also settled in the soul of my mother, Elsie Griffin Foy, from her Christian experiences in First Baptist Church of Roanoke, Virginia. When she moved to Winston-Salem in 1953 to become a music educator, her vocation led her to seek a Baptist congregation that worshiped God with the songs of Zion. Subsequently, First Baptist Church in East Winston-Salem was the place where she would "cast her lot." The annual performances of George F. Handel's *Messiah* and the musical anthems, favorite hymns, and Negro spirituals enabled her to celebrate God while perfecting her God-given gift as a soprano vocalist. When my parents came together to become one in 1957 as a result of meeting as music teachers in the Winston-Salem/Forsyth County Schools, their expression of faith was already one, one in Christ and one in the Baptist tradition—a perfect marriage.

First Baptist Church is the place where I, too, was inspired to celebrate God in song and in spirit. It is the place where I learned my ABCs in the kindergarten as a toddler, memorized Scripture as a child, was challenged to discover God as a preteen, and later was encouraged to become a lifelong student of the Bible as an adult. Like so many, I was perhaps a cultural Christian until I accepted Christ as my personal Savior at the age of eleven and was immersed in the baptismal pool as an outward sign of my confession of faith.

I was also taught at an early age that God was not Baptist, nor was Jesus black like me, nor was John the Baptist the founder of our Baptist denomination. I remember vividly the many discussions about John the Baptist and his purpose as the ambassador for Christ. Lessons on personalities of the Bible, the history of Baptists, and our beginnings as an African-American congregation in particular were rigorously taught to youth and adults alike. Leaders at various levels were developed both for ministry and for the community at large. Through weekly Sunday School, Baptist Training Union (BTU), Vacation Bible School, and the entire Board of Christian Education and Missions program, my framework for ministry was beginning to take shape. In essence, I was "preparing to be about my Father's (and forefathers') business."

My identity as a Baptist is perhaps more pertinent now as an adult than it was as a child. The more I have grown and witnessed many of God's blessings and even several of life's crises, the more I have grown in the Lord. Out of necessity the more I have understood who I am in Christ primarily through the study of scripture and prayer, the more liberated I have become to experience and expound to others what his love and grace provide.

As a college administrator, I have observed an increase in the expressions of personal spirituality, particularly over the past few years. Many of my students and colleagues have had challenging encounters. Some have struggled with the faith question of "Who is God, and what purpose does He have for my life?" Perhaps because I have never hidden the source of my faith or the context in which I worship, several have sought my counsel for some degree of direction. Subsequently, I have found myself in the vineyard of higher education, evangelizing from the very principles I know best—the Baptist viewpoint. My various administrative positions throughout my career have enabled me to interact with thousands of students—both enrolled and prospective. As a spiritual mentor to countless students and staff, I have also encouraged many who likewise have accepted the call to ministry.

In an age when people are free to exercise their choices, many Christians have elected to affiliate with other denominations. Contrary to some, I have never denied my Baptist allegiance, had an interest in transferring to another religious community, or been embarrassed by the caricature of Baptists that seems to be prominent in our society. Rather, the word Baptist symbolizes strength, unity, and freedom—an extension of my own personal rich heritage. I continue to believe that the Baptist heritage serves a vital role today for the following reasons.

First, perhaps Proverbs 22:6 is paramount to why I am still a Baptist. I am convinced that if we commit ourselves to training up children in the way they should go (in the Baptist culture), then maybe they will not consider leaving the denomination (or even God's presence) once they become old enough to make their own decisions. Certainly this basic principle is evident in my life and in the lives of my ancestors.

Second, I still believe that the Baptist tradition provides the most comprehensive, holistic approach to Christianity of any denomination that exists in our society. Baptist believers have always been a people of deliberate fellowship, discipleship, worship, leadership, and stewardship. These five "ships of Zion" have been our hallmark, encouraging us to sail through life as we apply these principles daily.

Third, I still believe that the flexibility and profound wisdom within our doctrinal structure, which was guided by the practice of the Baptist church of former days, retains its sufficiency as we endeavor to meet the needs of our day. In other words, the same Baptist teachings that encouraged my great-grandfather to challenge the social structure provided the encouragement for my grandmother to hold fast to her faith as she preached from her porch. Likewise, these same Baptist beliefs empower me to emulate my parents as servant leaders in the educational community.

For years the Baptist culture has served as surrogate parents for families and the entire community, especially among African-Americans. I am convinced that the Baptist culture, having made the greatest stance for civil rights, continues to enable persons of African descent to have an institution by which leadership is developed and encouraged. I still believe that the Baptist culture since its beginnings has maintained a commitment to Christian education that is transferable to the greater educational community. I still believe that the Baptist culture provides the most secure Christian foundation for young and not-so-young alike. And I will always believe that the Baptist culture has merit in our current society and for many generations to come.

As I commemorate the journeys of my ancestors, it is imperative that I simultaneously acknowledge the instrument that empowered their faith—the Baptist heritage. The Christian foundation my family members respected continues to have relevance today. I recognize that the challenge before me is to remember what it took for my forebears to persevere. Society will require that I make what happened one hundred years ago valuable for the years to come. Needless to say, I recognize that I stand on the shoulders of notable giants of faith, each of whom was empowered and nurtured by the Baptist tradition.

In the nineteenth century ours was a Baptist denomination that provided a structure to address social injustices. In the twentieth century ours is a Baptist denomination that provides a structure that demands equal rights. In the twenty-first century ours will be a Baptist denomination that provides a structure that fully embraces the true essence of God for all people—white, black, male, female, young, old, rich, poor.

Finally, as I prepare to enroll in the inaugural class at Wake Forest University School of Divinity, I endeavor to remain mindful of the rich legacy of my divine faith. Among the several theological programs across the country in which I might receive quality ministry training, it is of utmost importance that I study at Wake Forest University in Winston-Salem, North Carolina, my hometown.

As the first Southern private school to desegregate, Wake Forest University has experienced its own challenges as a Baptist institution, including its relationship to the Southern Baptist Convention. This fall, however, the university will enhance its original mission of training ministers. The new divinity school will be an academy that will honor one's walk of faith, the value of women in ministry, the Christian tradition, an ecumenical perspective, and most importantly the Baptist heritage.

Perhaps no one anxiously awaits the opening of the new school of divinity more than I. I have grown to appreciate the value of my family's faith lineage and my responsibility to keep the torch illuminated. I am compelled to pursue Wake Forest University for ministry training because of what their invitation will represent. Likewise, I trust that others have come to appreciate my sincerity for welcoming such an ambitious challenge at this stage of my life.

Like John the Baptist, God has commissioned me as His servant-leader to point people to Jesus Christ. My commitment to God and my concern for God's people empower me to accept the most humbling assignment I have ever encountered. I see the need to serve God, the Baptist church, and the educational community by answering the call, "Here I am, send me" (Isa 6:8).

Perhaps I may never be an eloquent preacher like my great-grandfather, a biblical scholar like my grandmother, or a master teacher like my father. My aspiration is simple: to serve God diligently, proclaiming His light to a darkening world in academia; to yield to the Spirit as I share the legacy of my divine faith; and to live every day of my life as Jocelyn the Baptist!

With All the Saints

Carole "Kate" Harvey

Kate Harvey

Why I am a Baptist today has to do with where I came from and where I believe creation is destined to arrive, and with the saints who have helped me along the way and those who will stand beside me at the end. The journey begins with the grace that lies over and around us every second of our lives and before and beyond, and that is still there at the end, even eternally.

When I was a child I did not have the words to theologize about this fundamental, foundational truth. The word "grace" was not in my vocabulary. My family was not a churchgoing family. But I did have a grandmother who loved me unconditionally and who told me the stories of Jesus as God's everlasting love, love that never lets us go, love willing even to die for us. What she said she lived out, enfleshing and enfolding me so completely in grace that the truth of it grabbed hold of me until the yearning grew within to make of my life something beautiful for God. Thank God for the grandmothers and grandfathers in the faith, whether or not they were our biological grandparents, who have blessed us all our lives and set us on the journey. But we need more than one person to tell us about Christ; we need the church, the body of Christ.

The time came when I was still a child, yet old enough to start going to church to seek out this God whose love had come seeking me in Jesus Christ. I began to attend Sunday school and worship services at the neighborhood Methodist church. I loved everything about it, descending the steps to the musty basement where children heard the ancient stories of our faith, reading the brilliantly-colored words on the chalkboard that proclaimed "God is love," standing to sing hymns with the adults upstairs in the grown-up church, growing up just enough myself to sing with the youth choir, even listening to some sermons that sounded rather boring to young ears and for all I knew to bored adults. I loved it all. I could not get enough of it.

You know how Methodists can enter the church through confirmation at about the age of twelve, after they are baptized as infants, sort of reversing the Baptist way of dedicating infants and baptizing teenagers. You can imagine how at that age everything in my being cried out to participate in those celebrations that would acknowledge God's gracious hold on my life and establish me in the household of grace. Can you imagine the grief when my parents refused me permission even to be baptized? It was probably because they felt that to agree would give the church permission to meddle in their home. So, on that glad and glorious day of confirmation I was absent from the procession as my friends made their way to the front of the church to speak their vows and to be received. I was invited to sing with the adult choir that day, because the rest of the youth choir was standing front and center to be welcomed into the next phase of their faith pilgrimage. From my place in the choir chancel I observed it all, singing the hymns with a broken heart, excluded from the home where I knew I belonged, unbaptized, unconfirmed, yet held in grace that would never let me go.

Each of us tells a different story of seeking God, who seeks us eternally. God is constant and holds on no matter where we are. During high school lunch hours my quest continued in yet another church, in the dark and empty sanctuary of the church across the street from school. I went there to meet God in the hushed holiness humming with the vibrations of the cloud of witnesses who had worshiped there throughout the years and even the Sunday before, whose faces I never saw because I lived too far from school and that church to walk there on Sunday. There I was, looking and longing for God, without the body of Christ to enflesh God's ways with humanity, to enfold me in church.

In college I met briefly for instruction with a priest from the Catholic tradition, which my father had abandoned when he married outside of it. Although I half expected to find my place in the tradition that had shaped him, I did not find my home there. As a young adult, thirty-four years ago, just after my daughter was born, I was baptized in a Presbyterian church where the family would gather a few weeks later for her Easter christening. Finally, in the fullness of time, the journey brought me to a Baptist church where at last I knew myself to be at home.

Here is how it came to pass. Moving from Cincinnati, Ohio, to Providence, Rhode Island, twenty-some years ago, my imagination was full of Roger Williams, founder of that city and father of the principle of separation of church and state. That he had had anything to do with Baptists had not yet come fully to my attention, nor had I ever thought much about Baptists as a whole. American Baptists in particular had not even crossed my radar, shocking as this confession may be to lifelong Baptists.

On the first Sunday in Rhode Island, the quaint colonial meeting house on the green summoned me with an almost mystical tug to come and worship. As weeks passed, remembering why I had never felt quite at home in the Presbyterian church I had been attending, with its double-predestination explanations of election, I asked everyone there what Baptists believe about election. The response was mostly blank stares, until the day when someone had the perfect answer: "What we believe about election is that you cannot vote until you join the church." And so I did, embracing the autonomy of the local church held forever in tension with the associational principle. Thus began the next phase of the journey, which took me in rapid succession into seminary and through a series of miraculously opened doors, ultimately to be the pastor of the church Roger Williams founded in 1638 and to my current position as Executive Director of the Ministers Council of the American Baptist Churches USA.

Along the way it has been my privilege to serve the denomination in a number of capacities, including the vice presidency in 1994–1995. As much as I cherish the saints I have known in the three American Baptist churches of my intimate acquaintance, within the larger body I have witnessed something greater: the unfolding of a denominational destiny that resonates profoundly with my deepest, dearest theological convictions and hopes. By the grace of God, not through anyone's intentional doing, we have come to prefigure the circle of saints at the end of time, red and yellow, black and white, precious in the sight of God and of one another.

Heaven as envisioned in Revelation 4 and 5 is imaged as concentric circles and crescendoing choirs, with God and the Lamb Jesus Christ at the center drawing everyone near. The closer each is to the center, the closer all are to sisters and brothers alongside. Saints from "all nations, every language, tribe, and people"—or at least many of them—have found a home in American Baptist churches, where the Baptist way of grace makes space for all to stand together. The task before us now is to become functionally what we have become numerically, the whole people of God, a body with tables of worship and work where all the saints are able to glorify God together.

In this day tensions tear at us just as at other denominations, threatening our capacity to hold on to one another as we hold on to the gospel. Some of us believe that faithfulness to the gospel requires us to draw the circle of belonging small and exclusive. Others of us believe that because the gospel assures room for all, faithfulness calls us to hold on to one another as we wrestle to discern the meaning of God's Word for us here and now. I believe that the way beyond impasse is to focus first and foremost not on who does or does not belong within the circle but on Jesus Christ, the center who summons and who makes possible the circle of humanity across all the ways we are different. If we first turn our eyes upon Jesus, then in the light of his glory and grace turn our eyes upon one another, American Baptists just may find our way through current impasses to the destiny God has set before us.

The question sometimes occurs to me: Why bother? Why has God so saturated my soul with the passion for holding on, that I am pouring out what seems to me the prime of my life for this small body of saints called American Baptists? Something in the depths of my soul responds with the recognition that nowhere else have I felt the foretaste of God's reign as surely as I do when we gather in our magnificent array of hues and tongues to worship God, and the glory of God is reflected in the richness of the many ways we bear God's image. The power in our togetherness arises not from the reverberations of the homogeneous unit principle, but from the filling and flowing of the Holy Spirit across our differences. What stirs us at such moments is manifestly not our sameness but God's Spirit. In this world I have experienced nothing like that reality, and for the sake of it I remain an American Baptist despite the death knells sounding the demise of denominations, and despite the dissensions within. Short of heaven, I do not know where else to seek the hope of a body becoming the whole people of God together.

That is my story, at least until today, Baptist through and through whether by accident or God's design. I value my baptism as an adult old enough truly to understand and yearn for it, the adult baptism that theoretically guarantees a regenerate church membership, even though too often our behavior with one another is more degenerate than anything. I value the autonomy and the interdependence that together are Baptist hallmarks, although it remains a struggle to live in the tension of soul liberty and communal discernment. I value who God is leading us to be together, even as I question how and even whether we are capable of arriving at that destiny.

I remember as a child playing Scrabble with my brother, quarreling every step of the way over which words were acceptable according to the rules that sometimes seemed too ambiguous and at other times too stringent, judgments determined by who benefited in each case. On one of those occasions our dear sainted grandmother overheard our disgraceful behavior. Finally, unable to bear it any longer, she commented, "The name of the game is Scrabble, not Squabble."

Sometimes listening to the squabbling of Baptists as we seek to establish the rules by which we do church together, I imagine the God who came in Jesus Christ to draw us near to God and each other listening in. At such times I imagine God saying, "Don't you get it? The name of the game is not Squabble; it is grace so amazing that I have poured out the life of my only Son to invite everyone who lives and moves and has being into the household of faith."

You see, I had not one grandmother but two, both named Beatrice Mae, both shown in photographs as young women with hauntingly sweet faces strikingly alike, only one of whom I ever knew. The other shut out her son, my father, and his new wife from a different faith tradition, along with three babies eventually born into the family, because she believed that the rules of her faith obligated her to exclude from her household anyone who saw truth differently than she.

I became a Baptist because I believed that here the wideness of God's mercy makes room for all in one household. As Roger Williams said when he established the city of Providence and the First Baptist Church in America, "Here is a place for all persons distressed of conscience." I remain a Baptist as long as there is hope that here all the saints of God can stand together and struggle together and strive together for that day when we shall know as we are known, and all things shall be made new.

Formation, Conviction, and Gratitude

— *Brian Haymes* —

B. Haymes

There are two different but related reasons that explain why I am a Baptist. They are matters of upbringing and conviction. The best way to explain all this, not least for theological reasons, is by way of autobiography. Any Baptist engaged in saying why she or he holds Baptist convictions will necessarily be involved in personal testimony.

I was born in 1940. Within days of my birth my father, a devout Anglican Christian, went to the war and served overseas. My mother promptly left their rented apartment in London and returned to her family home in Dorset to live with my grandparents. My mother, her parents, and most of my aunts and uncles were Baptists. It was among these people that I spent my first six years.

We worshiped with the local Baptist congregation, and from my earliest days at home and in church I was taught the stories of the Bible and heard of the love of the Christlike God. Those may have been war years, but I grew up secure, surrounded by people who loved me and whom I came to trust for their faithfulness. They did not argue about the authority of the Bible, but they followed Jesus, and their devotion and selfless service impressed me. All of this and more developed in me a growing childlike gratitude for Jesus Christ. I have come to count my Christian home as one of the gracious gifts God gave me.

When my father returned from the war, we went back to London. Immediately my parents joined the local Baptist church. By English standards it was a large congregation. I was quickly welcomed into the Sunday School and youth organizations.

Four things in particular I remember about the church: the powerful Christ-centered preaching; the deep quality of worship, where only the best would do because it was for God; the love and trust in the fellowship, which enabled young minds to inquire and question without being put down or driven out; and a sense that the very existence of the church was for the purposes of God in the world. It was at times thrilling to be among such people.

The call of Christ Jesus the Savior was often sounded in worship and youth groups. Yet I can never remember anyone's trying to force me or scare me into the Kingdom. However, I do recall one Sunday when I heard the invitation of Christ personally. My parents later told me that they knew something had happened at church because I was so unnaturally quiet. That evening, alone in my room, I gave my life to Christ. I told my parents early the next morning and went later in the day to tell the minister of my decision and to ask for baptism and church membership.

I knew from the biblical teaching I had received already and from the intensity of the inner experience, that the commitment to follow Jesus was the crucial decision of my life. I also knew that to be a member of Christ's church was a great privilege because the church was important in God's mission. That meant baptism was not simply my act alone, but was a part of the calling of a people by God, Father, Son, and Holy Spirit. I had much more to learn, but there was this early glimpse that baptism was amazingly into the life and mission of God.

So I was baptized and became a member of the church, a Baptist Christian. I was aware that there were other "types" of Christians, not least because the school I attended had an Anglican foundation. I recall the experience of being the only dissenter in the class when the chaplain supposed we would all be prepared for confirmation! I compared that approach to being the Christian church with what I had been taught from the Bible and found it wanting. I had become a Baptist, a consequence of upbringing and personal conviction.

The minister, members of the church, and others encouraged me to seek the life of service to which Christ was calling. I began preaching in my teenage years, mentored by two experienced local pastors. Eventually I came to believe I was called to be a minister. The local church and the London Baptist Association tested that call, and I entered Bristol Baptist College, the oldest continuing Baptist college in the world, to prepare for ministry.

In college I found among staff and students a passionate commitment to Jesus Christ, a deeply biblical scholarship that was open in the search for truth and pursued in the service of the gospel. It was a community of disciples. We had substantial disagreements on issues of theology and morals, but we trusted one another to be working with integrity at the faith by which we lived. This provided a secure place of freedom to explore the meaning of God's call and gift in Jesus. It was a Baptist place for theological engagement and personal formation.

Eventually I was called to a local pastorate, and so was ordained. Like being baptized, I have never quite come to terms with the privilege of being a Christian minister. All this is how and why I am a Baptist.

Why do I stay a Baptist? All through my ministry in pastorates and colleges I have been involved in ecumenical relationships. I have valued these for two reasons.

First, I have never believed that any one group of Christians knows all there is to know of God in Christ. This is true even of Baptists! So I have been grateful to listen and to learn with others who are seeking the unity Christ wills and gives to his people.

Second, I believe Baptists have important things to contribute to the understanding and proclamation of the Christian faith. The effect of all of this ecumenical engagement, so my friends tell me, is to make me more aggressively a Baptist than I was! I can believe that, for it is in the context of question and open debate that we come to clear our minds and appreciate our heritage. I have never understood the nervousness of those Baptists who stand outside the ecumenical quest. We have something important to bring, not least the vital gospel insights that keep me a Baptist.

Historically, the doctrine of the church has been the distinctive emphasis of Baptists. From within our ecclesiology I want to underline four things in particular. However, may I at this point remind the reader that I am a European? I live in the home of the Enlightenment, which has led to a society into which the acids of secularism and atheism have bitten deeply. In this context the churches I know best are called to live out the life in Christ. It is my conviction that the four

Baptist insights I shall emphasize are particularly crucial for the life
and mission of the church. These are not the only Baptist emphases,
but they are ones that strike me with particular significance at the
moment.

First, I am a Baptist because I believe in God, Father, Son, and Holy
Spirit. I believe in Jesus the Son of God who died for us all in sacrificial
saving love. I believe that Jesus was raised from the dead. I believe that
Jesus Christ, he and none other, is the one to whom all authority in
heaven and on earth has been given. He is Lord!

Moreover, I believe that an important part of the whole story of
Jesus is his calling of women and men to be his disciples and live the
life of his kingdom. I believe that Jesus Christ still calls women and
men to be the church today.

Baptists belong in the believers' church tradition. The church is
gathered first and foremost by the gracious call and invitation of the
Lord. The church is not built around or on some powerful personality,
however famous he or she may be in the cause of Christ. Neither is the
church a company of people whose assembly point is a specific doctrinal position, however soundly the doctrine might be stated. The origin
and heartbeat of the church is the call of God, and those who are its
members have by grace heard that call and responded to it in faith.
With and in Christ they are a fellowship of believers. Jesus Christ,
crucified and risen, is the one and only foundation God has laid.

This means that church membership is not a casual, optional extra.
Neither is it a matter of having the right parents or of being born into
a particular nation or culture. It has everything to do with God's saving
call in Jesus. It is not because I hold to some philosophical theory of
voluntarism that I am a Baptist, but because I believe that Jesus Christ,
the living Lord, calls and gathers his church.

Church membership is a great privilege. As Thomas Helwys put it
in 1611, "The church of Christ is a company of faithful people, separated from the world by the word and Spirit of God, being knit unto
the Lord and unto one another by baptism upon their confession of
the faith and sins" (spelling modernized). Thus, the church is not a
human option so much as a divine intention. That it has members is
from first to last a work of grace.

Second, as the quotation from Helwys indicates, we come to baptism. If the church is made up of those who have heard the call of God and responded in trusting faith, and if baptism is the scriptural sign of initiation into the church, then baptism is for believers only. That is the route Baptists take, from Christ, to church, to baptism into Christ, even into the life of God. Our emphasis on the personal call of Jesus Christ is underlined in baptism. No one can be baptized for another. No one should be baptized who has not freely responded to Christ in repentance and faith. Thus, the essential mission task of proclaiming the good news of God's salvation in Christ, of laying before people the crucial challenge and choice that belongs to the Kingdom of God, is affirmed.

Although baptism is personal, it is no private deal with Jesus. As a Baptist, I do not subscribe to individualism. Every occasion of baptism is a church event. Baptism is much more than an act of individual witness, or a mere symbol, as some say. It is an engagement with the triune God, a response to God who meets with us in our obedient response to his call. In baptism we are made a member of his church. We become sisters and brothers with all those others God has called and given us. We become part of the new humanity, which does not regard people primarily with the gender, economic, racial, or educational distinctions the world makes. We do not choose these sisters and brothers because, like us, they are in the church only by grace. We are gifts from God to each other. We are certainly in error if ever we divorce baptism from church membership.

I have never understood why Baptists are wary of a "sacramental" understanding of baptism. Why have we allowed sacramentalists to rob us of the truth that every baptism of a believer is a God-appointed "rendezvous," a meeting with God for all the church?

The God of the Bible hardly calls on us to perform empty gestures or mere symbols with nothing in them save what we humans bring. I believe that we Baptists at times come very near to selling baptism, even Christ himself, short when we reduce baptism to a privatized, spiritualized sphere. We are baptized into the name of the Father, the Son, and the Holy Spirit, into the fellowship of believers who have heard God's call and live as the new humanity in Christ. We are baptized into the life and mission of God, Creator, Savior, and Enabler.

Now, my third point. If Jesus Christ is the one to whom absolute authority in heaven and on earth has been given, then all other claims to authority are relativized. This includes any claims of the state. Again I recall the early Baptist, Thomas Helwys, making the first plea in the English language for religious freedom for all. His argument was not based on a philosophical theory about human rights, but was powerfully theological. It had to do with the sovereignty of God revealed in Jesus. For Helwys, Jesus Christ is the Lord. In him we are set free to be his followers, to live the life of his kingdom. This does not deny the proper claims that any state lawfully might make on its citizens, but it does put those claims into a certain context. It relativizes them.

In Christ the church is free to be the church under his rule. This remains an urgent argument in our contemporary world where church, state, nationhood, culture, and identity can all be compounded into a demanding and sometimes totalitarian whole. In the last analysis only God can tell His people how to worship, live, and serve. The gospel paradox to which Baptists have borne a sometimes costly witness is that only the sovereignty of the Christlike God can safeguard the freedom of the people. To stifle dissent in religion is potentially to set about stoning the prophets. I am glad of the Baptist stand for freedom, not as an absolute in itself but as the gift of the liberating God.

Properly, all our church meetings and assemblies are about a common seeking of the mind of Christ the Lord. When we are more concerned about winning votes for our self-declared goals, we are not living as the church of Christ. At their best, Baptists have a lot to teach others about how to have divided opinions within a common loyalty. Religious freedom, with the concept of a free church in a free state, is an important Baptist conviction.

So to my last point. Early English Baptists were properly concerned with "right belief." They carefully wrote confessions in which they declared their theological convictions and doctrinal affirmations. They used those confessions to teach, defend, and explain themselves to others. This is always an urgent and proper task for the church. It requires loving God with all our minds. But early Baptists knew these were their work, human words, a confession of faith for their time. They did not write creeds.

This has always seemed to me to be a matter of real spiritual wisdom. Creeds define the church doctrinally. Baptists define the church just as much in relational terms, preeminently with Christ. The sign of a living relationship with Jesus the Lord is not first an ability to recite sound words, but is faithful active discipleship. Indeed, by their fruits you shall know them. Again, what is being affirmed is the final absolute authority of Jesus Christ, the living word. All of our words, even our best human utterances and scripts, only approximate to him who is the truth. The test is not only whether we hold acceptable views on doctrine, but also whether in trusting love we follow the Lord. After all, Jesus said that calling him "Lord, Lord" was not in itself the way of the kingdom. That was all about doing the will of God. Baptists have always set doctrine and discipleship together.

These, then, are some of the aspects of the various Baptist traditions I value and that keep me a Baptist, even while I am conscious of the urgent mission call in the ecumenical vision. I do not deny that other Christians may affirm some or all of these. But I do claim that there is a way of being church that is Baptist, that holds these together and tries to be faithful to the Bible. This way is different from Catholicism, Orthodoxy, and even Protestantism. It is being Baptist. And with, I hope, an open-minded modesty, that recognizes that not even the Baptist word is final, I shall be glad to go on affirming such things until Christ leads us beyond the ways known to those yet to be made known.

Why I Am Still a Baptist

Margaret B. Hess

The explanation of why I am a Baptist is in some ways a simple one: I was born to parents who were members of a Baptist church. My father started out as a Methodist, but my mother was a Baptist and her mother before her. My little white leather New Testament, whose Gospel of John I colored with a red crayon at some point in my development, has a front page slathered with Scotch tape. Beneath the yellowed tape it is written that on May 12, 1957, I was dedicated to God by L. D. Johnson, the pastor of our church. I was a fat, bald baby. In my mind's eye I can see my parents hefting their ten-month-old into Dr. Johnson's arms, who leaned his own bald head toward mine while saying some holy words over me, after which everyone smiled. He then handed me back to my parents, but his blessing was just the beginning of my welcome into the fold called Baptist.

Memory. I am quite small, and I stand on my tiptoes to reach up over the lower half of the Dutch door in the church nursery. Miss Sally, her white curls neatly combed in place, leans down to kiss my head. She coos and clucks and calls us her babies. She smells of powder and perfume, and her hands are bone thin as she pats me on the head.

Memory. The water is colder than I expect, and my white robe swims around me as the preacher takes my hand and leads me into the baptistery. I take a deep breath and am plunged into the uterine waters of baptism. I come up for air and am never the same again.

Memory. Wednesday night church suppers: chicken, mashed potatoes, gravy, green peas, biscuits. We all talk and laugh, and then someone rises and tells us about what is happening on the mission field.

Memory. I stand with twenty girls in the dark on the edge of our cabin porch at Camp Viewmont. The beam of a flashlight swings through the night and lights up our porch, and we all sing: "Day is done . . ." I think again of the missionary story we heard in the chapel that day, and wish I could grow up to be as brave as Lottie Moon.

A net of memory was cast over me, and in retrospect I see that all of these recollections are deeply Baptist.

If early experience was not enough to make a Baptist of me, then there was always incarnation, memory's co-conspirator. Becoming a Baptist was an incarnational operation. I knew what it meant to be a Baptist because others embodied Baptist principles or ideals in my presence. Dr. Johnson was just the first in a long line of Baptists who taught me about the primacy of Jesus Christ and the importance of scripture as a guide to the life of faith in Christ. I sat through many sermons as a child, no doubt coloring my way through the Gospels, until one day I woke up in the middle of a sermon.

I was in third grade, and the visiting preacher quoted a poem: "I saw God wash the world last night. . . ." The preacher had captured my imagination. I began to make connections between what the preacher had to say and what I felt inside. I began to think my way through the stories of faith that I had heard over and over. Scripture had become a living, breathing thing, and so had this Jesus I had heard so much about.

I knew who Jesus was through the Scriptures, and others helped me to access the vitality of the Bible and a living faith in Christ. Luke Smith preached about Jesus, and I began to understand the connections between faith and responsibility. In my introduction to the New Testament course Roger Crook explained about "Q" and the synoptic Gospels, and suddenly I was alive with a hunger to know everything I could discover about the Bible and its formation as sacred canon. Larry Williams, my college chaplain, listened for hours as I began to puzzle my way through an emerging call to ministry. His attentive presence taught me about soul freedom and how to discern where my own relationship with Jesus would lead me. The centrality of Jesus, the primacy of scripture, soul freedom: these principles were embodied in people who loved me with great patience and kindness. Baptist ideals came to me clothed in flesh and bone, an incarnational faith.

So that is how I came to be a Baptist, through this conspiracy of happenstance, memory, and incarnation. But, of course, we all know that being a Baptist is a matter of *choice*, not chance. We are not *born* Baptist. We do not become Baptist by accident or default. We *elect* to be a Baptist. Which brings me to the second part of this essay. Why am I still a Baptist? That is another question altogether, and a more complicated one.

I sit at one of the heavy wooden tables in the refectory of the College of Preachers, sipping my tea and listening to the after-dinner conversation. I am the only Baptist in a group that is predominantly Episcopalian. One after another my colleagues tell how they came to be Episcopalian. One had been ordained Methodist, another Presbyterian, but in time they saw the light and sought out Episcopalian ordination as a matter of choice and principle. Suddenly a wild thought crosses my mind. "Maybe I could become an Episcopalian," I muse out loud. "I like the Episcopalians. You are so *precise*; Baptists are so *messy*." One of my colleagues laughs and says: "The only difference is that we write everything down." To tell the truth, I cannot imagine being anything other than Baptist. And besides, I do not think I could survive another defection.

I had been in seminary for two years when I made the decision to become an American Baptist. I felt disloyal leaving the Southern Baptist Convention, as if I were rejecting my own flesh and blood. But my call to ministry had taken a surprising turn, and I found myself seized by a growing conviction that I was called to preach. With that conviction came the uneasy awareness that it would be difficult, if not impossible, to live out that call within a Southern Baptist culture. The storm clouds were gathering on the denominational horizon, and I sensed that I had to choose my battles carefully. I knew that ministry would be difficult enough for me in a supportive context and next to impossible in a setting where conferred authority might be withheld. And so I chose to cast my lot with the American Baptist Convention. The choice was a good one for me, but I always felt sad that such a sacrifice seemed necessary. The sense that I was defecting was accompanied by an awareness of deficit. It would be years before I was convinced that the deficit was not within me, but in a system that could not fully embrace the ministries of women.

Looking back, I see that there were a number of choices available to me in 1980 regarding my denominational commitment. I chose to remain Baptist for a variety of reasons, the least of which was to retain a sense of continuity with my original faith context. There were other obvious distinctives that held me: the emphasis on religious liberty, believer's baptism, the priesthood of all believers, the autonomy of the local congregation. But there was another pivotal piece of this puzzle, one that even now is harder to articulate. It had something to do with seeking wholeness in the context of diversity. Over time I have come to think of diversity as one of the great gifts and burdens of being Baptist. My attraction to diversity remains a mysterious charism that keeps me firmly committed to the soul freedom that Baptists profess.

In my estimation, Baptists have a pretty shaky track record on the matter of diversity. We say we are committed to soul freedom, but then things tend to fall apart when we try to live it out in the real world. We say we honor a believer's right and responsibility to reach one's own theological conclusions, but then we get nervous when others' conclusions differ from our own. The historical record shows that Baptists too often have opted for rigidity over openness, dogma over confessions of faith, and narrow viewpoints over a capacity to think creatively on theological issues. Unfortunately, Baptists have been impoverished by such trends.

Some of my most profound spiritual struggles and growth have been centered around trying to remain in community with people with whom I have more differences than similarities. I often wonder: "How much difference can a relationship tolerate and still remain intact?" This is one of the many questions Baptists face today. I believe it is our call to sort this question out in a faithful manner.

A genuine commitment to soul freedom requires both the ability to state clearly one's position and a capacity to tolerate anxiety when distance is created between two perspectives. Through my tenure on the Executive Committee of the 168 National Ministers Council, I have had an intense firsthand experience of learning to sit with people whose feet are firmly planted on the other side of many issues. It is generally easier for me to hang around with people who agree with me than to be with people with whom I differ. I have continued to work at my relationships with my colleagues on the Ministers Council primarily because I feel a call from God to do so. Through honesty, hard work, tears, confrontation, openness, and the sheer grace of God, some amazing things have emerged.

I have discovered that I love these people with whom I differ. Our differences are legion: racial, ethnic, and cultural backgrounds; theological perspectives; sources of authority; goals and vision for ministry —to name only a few. But we have discovered a common ground that holds us together: the love of our compassionate Savior, Jesus Christ. The hard work of staking out a common place to stand is a valuable model for our denomination and for our world. . . . Which brings me again to the question "Why am I still a Baptist?"

I often come home from Baptist meetings feeling tired, angry, frustrated, and despairing. My husband asks, "So why *are* you still a Baptist anyway?" "Heaven only knows," I reply. There is a great deal of truth in that. But this much I do know: I am still a Baptist because I believe that in our struggle to live out the call to soul freedom in a faithful way, we offer a valuable gift to those around us. We live in a world that is increasingly complex and diverse, a world that needs models of how to reach beyond our tribal and theological differences in order to find ways to serve God and to work out the salvation of the human soul. In learning to embrace our rich diversity, Baptists have the opportunity to give the world such a gift. Perhaps we have come to the kingdom for a moment such as this.

As a Baptist, I work out my salvation in fear and trembling, and I live my faith in an odd gap. The gap lies between our espoused theology, which proclaims soul freedom, and our operative theology, with its tendency toward a rigid, fractured polarization of the body. Once in a great while the distance between our espoused and operative theology closes, and we find ourselves in a sacred moment of genuine community.

My vision of that place is something like a Baptist potluck. The table is laden with dishes that reflect the diversity around it: pot roast, tortillas, rice and beans, sushi, fried chicken, goulash, and the 170 Baptist deviled eggs. As I look around the table, I know in my heart that this is why I am still a Baptist. We talk and laugh and sing, with Christ in our midst. We are stunned by a joy so surprising, so mighty, that our cup overflows, and the mercy of God spills out all around us, flowing out into the world without end, amen.

Being Baptist
Hospitable Traditionalism
—— *Bill J. Leonard* ——

Bill Leonard [signature]

As I look back on twenty-five years of classroom teaching, I recall one particularly volatile moment when a class rose up against me, questioning my faith and commitment to Christian virtues. The issue, however, was not biblical authority or the doctrines of Christ's virgin birth, substitutionary atonement, or bodily resurrection. It did not involve questions of race, gender, or other controversial issues of twentieth-century theological and ethical life. It was about the American flag.

The incident occurred in Religion 103, Introduction to Religion, at Samford University in Birmingham, Alabama. In a lecture on civil religion I simply remarked that I could not belong to a congregation that "posted the colors"—displayed the American flag complete with Marine guard—at a 4th of July service or any other worship event in a Christian church. Such actions, I believe, crossed a line between primary honor to God and loyalty to an earthly state. And, I added, those convictions were passed on to me by the people called Baptists.

The students, many reared in Baptist churches, were incensed. They suggested that I was neither a good citizen nor a good Christian. As they saw it, objecting to a sincere effort to foster patriotism, respect for the American flag, freedom, and the role of religion in shaping the Republic was secular humanism at best, blatant heresy at worst. For many of the students, I had forsaken Christian identity for the sake of a mere denomination. One student asked: "Aren't we supposed to be loyal to Christ, not to a denomination?" Wasn't the effort to separate church and state exactly what was wrong with the "New Age" of American religious and political life? For many in the class, denominations were of human creation. True Christian identity meant simple trust in Jesus, belief in the authority of the Bible, and commitment to a basic nonsectarian, nondenominational, and "biblical" Christianity.

I think often about that exchange with my students, grateful for their willingness to take their professor to task about ideas and issues, and mindful that the class was a teachable moment for me—and I hope for them. It helped me to realize that certain Baptist "ways" have shaped me irrevocably and that I am, for better or for worse, a Christian whose ideas and convictions bear a discernibly Baptist twist. It was also a reminder that Baptists themselves cannot agree on what "being Baptist" involves.

Perched on the edge of the twenty-first century, claiming a Baptist identity may seem terribly out of date. Studies show that fewer and fewer religious Americans, and other world citizens, think of their primary religious identity in terms of a denominational identity. Many churches, including certain Baptist congregations, are dropping or at least minimizing denominational nomenclatures. Others simply call themselves "community churches," "people's churches," or "fellowships," in an effort to get beyond "brand-name religion" and longstanding denominational debates, divisions, and sectarianism. For many folks, especially in the American South, retaining the Baptist name is particularly problematic because of all the public controversy, caricatures, and insults that Southern Baptists have hurled at each other for decades. Given twenty years of abuse and argument, the name "Baptist" is not merely divisive; it is downright embarrassing.

While acknowledging obvious historical, psychological, and theological difficulties, I continue to call myself a Baptist Christian. In fact, as we race into the third millennium, I find myself particularly concerned to declare myself and explain what being a Baptist means for me. These days I fret over efforts to produce a kind of generic Christianity, since I am not sure that such a thing exists. Indeed, there is no truly generic Christianity, that is, Christianity without form, shape, history, tradition, and distinctiveness. In a sense all Christians share a core of common beliefs relative to faith. The Apostles' Creed captures those ideas wonderfully.

> I believe in God the Father Almighty, maker of Heaven and earth, and in Jesus Christ, his only Son, and our Lord. Who was conceived of the Holy Spirit, born of the Virgin Mary, suffered under Pontius Pilate, was crucified, dead, and buried. He descended into hell. On the third day he rose again from the dead. He ascended into Heaven. From thence he will come to judge the living and the dead. I believe in the Holy Spirit, the Holy Catholic Church, the Communion of Saints, the resurrection of the dead, and the life everlasting. Amen.

Yet those dogmas take on identity in concrete communities. No mention is made of baptism, the Supper, or the form of church polity. Even in the New Testament, Christianity takes on dramatic specificity in a variety of theological and geographical contexts. Christianity at Thessalonica—energized over the return of Christ—is distinct from that of Corinth—charismatic, argumentative, and (to St. Paul's chagrin) thriving. Likewise, the theologically inquisitive faith found at Rome is quite a contrast from the spiritually ethereal devotion evident in the church at Colossi. St. Paul wrote to them all about an encompassing faith, true enough, but never without an understanding of the context and the uniqueness present in each distinct community.

Christian traditions offer us a place to stand, a family that helps us understand who we are and where we fit in the pilgrimage of faith. Thus, I would opt for what might be called a "hospitable traditionalism," a source of identity that gives us a source of truth from which to continue the search for truth. It should turn us outward on the world, not inward on ourselves. My own commitment to Baptist ideals is formed around that understanding of a hospitable traditionalism, which, while grounded in Baptist identity, draws on a variety of traditions throughout the Christian church. I am forever indebted, for example, to Roman Catholics for guidance into spirituality, to two Methodist institutions—Texas Wesleyan and Boston Universities—for much of my higher education, and to holiness/Pentecostals for insights into Christian sanctification. Having a Baptist place to stand does not limit one to only Baptist ways of believing and acting.

Why take the name Baptist as a way of defining Christian identity? My reasons are complex and personal. From the beginning it is necessary to acknowledge that being a Baptist requires considerable humility and not a little qualification. On certain issues the Baptist family, like all Christian communities, has often come out on the back side of grace. Baptists, particularly the Anglo-Saxon, Southern, American variety, often find themselves weighed in the historical balances and found wanting on issues of dogma, race, and politics. Consider some of our very public mistakes.

Landmarkism, that effort to document a certain historical uniqueness by tracing Baptists all the way back to Jesus and the River Jordan, was a "made-up" history, concocted to do battle against other Christian denominations. It was a creative, though faux, method for demonstrating that Baptists alone were the one true church. While Baptists may be part of Christ's church, Landmarkism was not a historically credible means of proving the veracity of Baptist identity.

Likewise, Southern Baptists were, with a few notable exceptions, wrong on race. They were wrong on slavery and used the Bible to undergird their support of the South's "peculiar institution." Losing that battle, they were wrong on segregation, again utilizing Holy Scripture as a resource for preserving the racially discriminatory practices of a culture. They were also wrong on Catholics, at least in the claim that the election of a Catholic president—Al Smith or John F. Kennedy—would destroy American political and religious freedom. And, in my view, they have generally been wrong on women—the idea that God cannot possibly call a female to missionary service, the diaconate, pastoral ministry, and other forms of explicit Christian service. Thus, from certain historical and theological perspectives, one claims the name Baptist cautiously and not without some qualification.

Like any family, the Baptist communion is at points dysfunctional, having significant problems, blind spots, and sinfulness on issues theological and ethical. Similarly, Baptists are a huge family, given to multiple subdivisions, feuds, and irreconcilable differences. To be a member of the Baptist family, therefore, is to acknowledge that there is terrific diversity. Thus I prefer to speak, not of one clear-cut Baptist *way*, but of Baptist *ways*, confessing that there are multiple ways to be, believe, and act inside the Baptist rubric.

With those caveats, perhaps I can turn to my own reasons for claiming and retaining the name Baptist to describe my Christian identity. First, I am a Baptist because I started out that way.

Don't laugh. Christian nurture brought me into the Baptist family. Long before I entered the world, my parents had entered the Baptist fold. As a child, my father was baptized along with his mother, brother, and sister in a pond across the road from the cemetery (where his ashes now rest) in the little town of Paradise, Texas. My mother received similar baptism at Chico, Texas, some twenty miles outside Paradise.

My maternal grandmother, Frances Mowery Henton, was a long-time member of the Independent Fundamental Baptist Church of Decatur, Texas, a congregation allied with the "Texas Tornado," populist preacher J. Frank Norris, who left the Southern Baptist fold in the 1930s. Outside its doors stood a neon anchor that flashed the words "Jesus Saves" as a witness for all to see. Going to revivals with her as a child, I soon learned that my grandmother and her fellow fundamentalist Baptists had a one-sentence way of evaluating their preachers: "He don't sweat; we don't listen!" My grandmother Henton was one of the most grace-filled human beings I have ever known. She lived in our home for many years, and her strength of character, her gentleness, and her humility (she was also one tough woman) shaped me in ways I cannot now or perhaps ever decipher completely.

My parents and grandparents took me to Baptist churches almost from the moment I entered the world. God's grace sought me out in Baptist Vacation Bible Schools, revival meetings, and particularly in Sunday School classes at the First Baptist Church of Decatur, Texas, the town where I was born. I am a debtor to all the people in that congregation, particularly Sunday school teachers, who blessed me and lived out the gospel before my very eyes. I shall never forget the way they nurtured me to faith.

Recently I found my first New Testament, a gift from Miss Winnie Bradford, one of my first Sunday school teachers, a volume I received before I could even read. It was in another such class, one taught by Mr. Johnny Ramey, that I first heard, or remembered, the "plan of salvation," and in response claimed or was claimed by God's good grace. I received baptism in the eighth year of my life, administered in a Baptist baptistery with the Jordan River painted on the wall behind it.

Baptists, too many to name in this brief article, set me on the journey of faith, challenged me to make the church's faith my own, and offered care along the way. They set a Christian and Baptist identity in me so deeply that I cannot seem to let it go. I am a Baptist because I was nurtured into it.

Second, I am a Baptist because Baptist ways of believing and acting inform my continuing struggle for and with Christian faith. Yet those basic statements are themselves informed by the Baptist heritage. Baptist theology is certainly lively, though not necessarily consistent. Baptists are (selective) biblicists, conversionists, congregationalists, pragmatists, and controversialists, among other things, and that selectivity is especially evident in their theology.

Baptists begin at both ends of the theological spectrum, first in 1609 as Armenians, convinced that free will, general atonement, and the possibility for all are central to the biblical message. By the 1630s there were Calvinist Baptists, declaring that divine sovereignty, election, predestination, and limited atonement are the essential doctrines of Holy Scripture. Groups as diverse as the Primitive Baptists and the Free Will Baptists characterize Baptist history with innumerable communions somewhere in between. The Baptist family numbers among its members liberals and fundamentalists, slaveholders and abolitionists, Harry Emerson Fosdick and Jerry Falwell, Richard Furman and Howard Thurman, Dorothy Patterson and Molly Marshall.

Indeed, Baptist individuals, ideas, doctrines, and actions seem to exist in paradox, creating a fascinating and almost always divisive tension. For several years I have sought to understand so-called "Baptist distinctives," less as a systematic collection of individual beliefs than as a series of ideas connected in consistent paradox. These include the following.

Biblical Authority—Soul Liberty

Baptists are unashamed biblicists, utilizing Hebrew and Christian Scriptures as guides for faith, morals, doctrine, and practice. Even in constructing confessions of faith that set forth basic Baptist doctrines, most Baptists made certain that these ideas were not to have precedent over the written word of God. While recent Baptists have debated what the inspiration and authority of the Bible mean, they have not denied its important place in Baptist personal and communal life.

At the same time Baptists created a context by which individuals, under the guidance of the Holy Spirit and (generally) in the context of churchly community, might be trusted to read and interpret Scripture for themselves. While this radical idea never meant that one was free to be a Baptist and believe anything, it did suggest that the individual had a freedom and responsibility to read and struggle with the text of Scripture in powerful, dynamic, and, yes, divisive ways.

At its best, biblical authority keeps soul liberty from becoming antinomianism and rabid individualism, while soul liberty keeps biblical authority from becoming idolatry or, as the old preachers said, "corpse cold creedalism."

A Believer's Church

Born of nurture and spiritual catharsis, Baptists believe that all persons who claim Christian faith should testify in some way to having experienced directly and personally the saving grace of God in Christ. This is sometimes known as an evangelical conversion experience, being born again, being saved, trusting Christ, or accepting Jesus as your personal Savior and Lord.

From the earliest days of the Baptist movement (seventeenth-century Holland and Britain), Baptists have understood the church as a community of believers who have made an "adult profession of faith." (They got that idea from the Bible, the Radical Reformers, and the English Puritans.) Yet while they have called persons to experience conversion—often described as a dramatic salvific experience—they have not hesitated to nurture persons to faith from early age. Children are taught, blessed, and mentored into the Kingdom of God as readily as adults are urged to believe, repent, and be "saved."

In other words, Baptists, implicitly or explicitly, create multiple paths for discovering grace. Some testify to having said yes to grace in such small increments as if it had been there all along. Others declare a radical conversion by which they are suddenly and unexpectedly apprehended by grace, as if it had never been present before. Others claim elements of both. While the rhetoric of Baptists often seems only to promote radical and immediate conversion, their actions promote nurture of persons through a gentle process along the way to faith.

Word Enacted—Sacraments/Ordinances

Baptists are perhaps most identified with believer's baptism by immersion, the sacrament/ordinance for which many early Baptists were fined, imprisoned, and even martyred. Although the earliest Baptists did not discover immersion until some thirty years after they began, the practice has consistently been observed in all Baptist churches since the 1640s.

Baptism by immersion is a dramatic event that literally enacts the Word of God, symbolically plumbing the depths of death and resurrection, cleansing and new life. In baptism the individual believer is united with the whole church, past, present, and future. Baptismal immersion was, and to a certain extent remains, a controversial and dramatic element of Baptist identity. It is a profound moment in which faith is publicly professed in the presence of Christ and the believing community. Likewise, if baptism marks the beginning of faith, the Lord's Supper marks faith's journey. It is the sign of God's continuing presence and grace with God's people, the church.

These two sacraments/ordinances reveal something of Baptists' selective biblicism, however. For example, since the 1640s Baptists have emphasized the normative nature of baptism by immersion as the only biblical mode. Water is the baptismal norm for genuine Christian/biblical baptism. Yet, since the nineteenth century, Baptists, at least in the United States, have generally relinquished wine as the biblical norm for the Lord's Supper in favor of nonbiblical, temperance grape juice. Selective literalism is a continuing challenge for Baptist Christians.

Some Baptists also practice the washing of feet (John 13) as a sign of their servanthood to Christ and one another. While this act may not rank with the two other sacrament/ordinances, it is a powerful symbol that Baptist groups have long cultivated. I have participated in numerous footwashings over the years and am consistently struck at the power of this observance. So great is its impact on my own spiritual life that I do not hesitate to consider myself a "Footwashing Baptist."

Local Autonomy—Associational Cooperation

Baptists have long emphasized the autonomy of each local congregation and the ability of the people of God in one specific churchly setting to decide for themselves on matters of faith and mission. In this Baptists are unashamed congregationalists, believing that the authority of Christ is mediated through the believer's church. Yet from their very earliest times Baptists formed associations of churches and later denominational connections at local, regional, and national levels.

Again, Baptist polity suggests that the people can be trusted under God to determine the will of God for their work and worship. This relationship between localism and cooperation is a continuing tension for Baptists and has produced innumerable schism and splits at every level of denominational life. Local autonomy offers great freedom, but it also insures division as opinions and convictions clash. So, too, associational cooperation is always in tension with localism. The dynamics are powerful, energizing, and messy. From the beginning, Baptists created a system of governance and cooperation that not only anticipated conflict, but also guaranteed it.

Priesthood of the Laity—Calling Out Ministers

Like other Reformation-based Protestants, Baptists emphasize the priesthood of the laity, an idea closely related to a believer's church, individual conversion, and congregational autonomy. Not only was each person free to seek grace directly from Christ without formal mediation of ecclesiastical hierarchy or intercession, but conversion itself was a door to the mission and ministry of all believers.

Indeed, many early Baptists practiced the laying on of hands in two ways: they laid hands on every newly baptized Christian as a sign of the Holy Spirit and the calling that all persons received, and they laid hands on a specific group of persons set aside for ministers. Thus, they lived with the tension between a congregation of priests working alongside an ordained clergy.

Such an approach to ministry and mission can provide great resources, utilizing clergy and laity as "priests to each other" and to the world. It can also create great divisions in specific congregations and throughout Baptist denominational life as various groups struggle with the question, "Who is in charge?"

Cautiously Confessional—Selectively Creedal

Baptists wrote confessions of faith almost from the beginning of their movement. Those confessions, most of which were written in the seventeenth century, set forth basic dogmas in a systematic form. The confessions dealt with scripture, conscience, congregationalism, faith, church, baptism, the Supper, religious liberty, salvation, and other classic doctrines. Most were either Calvinist or Armenian in theological orientation and informed the type of Baptist individual or community that accepted them.

Many Baptists used these confessions cautiously, careful to insist that these documents were not to take precedence over Scripture or even individual conscience. They were used to establish doctrinal boundaries, nurture fellowship, and deal with heresy. At certain times the confessions became selectively creedal; that is, they were sources for dealing with unorthodox belief or confronting specific doctrinal controversies.

Confessionalism and creedalism alike have characterized innumerable Baptist controversies. Yet, given Baptist polity, confessions can be amended by majority vote, or can, by virtue of local autonomy and individual conscience, be reinterpreted, enforced, or ignored. Confessions inform Baptist identity significantly. Baptist polity makes their uses diverse, controversial, and limited.

Religious Liberty—Loyalty to the State

Next to baptismal immersion, perhaps Baptists have been known best for their rabid advocacy of radical religious liberty. In fact, seventeenth-century Baptists were the first to articulate in English a doctrine of absolute liberty of conscience, insisting that the state could not judge in matters of religion. God alone was judge of conscience, and the state could not punish the heretic or the atheist. Yet Baptists did not hesitate to affirm their loyalty to the state and their commitment to solid citizenship. Many of the earliest Baptist treatises on religious liberty were addressed to monarchs and magistrates, with the authors pleading for religious freedom, not as anarchists, but as loyal, concerned contributors to the best of ordered society.

As I read and reread the Baptists, it seems to me that they are at their best in defending the rights of persons and communities to absolute religious liberty. In a real sense it was Baptist-based Rhode Island, not Puritan Establishment Massachusetts, that anticipated religious America.

Community of Saints—Dissenting Individuals

Another paradox in Baptist life haunts me. It is the tension between the community and the individual. On one hand Baptists are bound to the community of the church. That community baptizes, ordains, celebrates the Supper, worships, and gathers around the word of God. Individual conversion has communal implications. Yet there are times when the individual chooses to stand against convention, prevailing opinion, the culture, and even the community for the sake of conscience and conviction.

The dissenting tradition of the Baptists is a haunting element of the history and identity of a people. To recount Baptist history is to tell the story of dissent. Thomas Helwys died in prison in 1616 (or thereabouts) because of his call for radical religious liberty. Roger Williams was exiled into the "howling wilderness" of New England because he would not accept the idea of a "Christian nation." "Swearing Jack" Waller (his preconversion name) was jailed in colonial Virginia because he would not secure a preaching license from the state. Walter Rauschenbusch called for a theology of the social gospel that would challenge the materialism and exploitation of the "robber barons." Martin Luther King, Jr., raised his voice against segregation from Baptist pulpits across the American South. The dissenters were vilified in their day, but their legacies shaped the community of faith, even when it was not recognized or appreciated. Dissent and community collide with some frequency in Baptist life, even as do the other elements of Baptist belief and practice.

✝✝✝✝

So I remain a Baptist, less because of the consistency than because of the messiness of this strange and wonderful heritage. I cannot make it all fit any more than I can make the gospel all fit into a nice package without contradiction, controversy, and occasional confusion. Recently, in an article I wrote on Baptist historiography, I tried to summarize something of the Baptist ethos. In a real sense it describes those ideas and issues that keep me a Baptist. It is a declaration of faith. Finally, on the way to the future, Baptists might remember and reexamine the ideas that gripped their unruly forebears. They might be summarized as follows:[1]

• There are many "ways" to be Baptist and many Baptist "stories" to be claimed.

• Ideas are worth fighting over.

• Dissent is a worthy pursuit.

• The Bible is the written Word of God.

• Jesus is the living Word of God.

• Faith is both personal and communal.

• Baptism and the Supper are life-changing, grace-filled moments that mark the Christian journey.

• The people can be trusted.

• God alone is judge of the conscience.

• Doctrines can and should be articulated by communities of faith.

• Controversy is inevitable.

• Religion at its best is not generic; it has specificity and peculiarity.

• Being a Baptist is messy, controversial, divisive, and energizing.

Note

[1]Bill J. Leonard, "Memory and Identity among Baptists in the South," in Ronald A. Wells, ed., *History and the Christian Historian* (Grand Rapids: Wm. B. Eerdmans Publishing Co., 1998) 136.

A Baptist by Conscience
A Baptist in Hope
——— *Molly T. Marshall* ———

I have always been one, you know. Being Baptist has basically been the same as being alive for me. Certainly it is more than being born into such an ecclesial legacy, but the formative power of that cannot be gainsaid. Christian heritage on my mother's side of the family was heavily weighted toward Baptist identity. Along with milk, I was nourished as a little child with stories of my great-grandfather, W. S. Wiley, a pioneer Baptist preacher in Indian Territory. Traveling on horseback through what is now northeastern Oklahoma, he worked with Cherokees, Choctaws, and Creeks as they sought together to start Sunday Schools and plant churches. Thus, my earliest impressions of Baptists had to do with proclamation of the gospel to all people. Baptists believed in missions, and sacrificial effort was a necessary part of adhering to the mandate of the Great Commission.

My father's uncle, Jasper Newton Marshall, who attended the Southern Baptist Theological Seminary at the turn of the century, was also a pioneer Baptist preacher. His ministry was primarily in central Texas, which led to his being dubbed "Prophet of the Pedernales." His autobiography recounts his wide-ranging preaching and educational ministry as Baptist work gained strength throughout Texas. From him I learned that churches need a great deal of tending, and helpful resources from theologically educated ministers were absolutely necessary.

Being Baptist was considered honorable by these forebears, a constructive and active way to offer their lives in faith and service. Our family revered early denominational statespersons, missionaries, and educators such as Ann and Adoniram Judson, Luther Rice, Lottie

Moon, E. Y. Mullins, A. T. Robertson, Walter Rauschenbusch, and our own Aunt Clema Wiley (who finished the WMU Training School in 1920), believing that their leadership was wise and godly.

Many years have passed since my early formation as a Baptist, and many difficult years have ensued in the Southern Baptist context. We are all deeply acquainted with grief and the rending pain of a dismembered family. Many of our brothers and sisters have felt that remaining Baptist was just too costly, and we must honor their liberty of conscience even as we grieve their departure.

So why am I still a Baptist after having my calling to ministry scrutinized and denounced repeatedly and finally being told I was "not trustworthy to teach theological students" at Southern Seminary? I have asked myself that question more than once in recent years when remaining Baptist seemed to ensure involvement in a protracted internecine "battle for the mind." Yet a Baptist I remain—out of conscience and hope.[1] In the next few pages of this brief article I will outline why the Baptist vision continues to claim my life and vocation.[2]

I am a Baptist committed to the contours of the believers' church tradition[3] that stands for (and on) religious liberty. Perhaps no other Baptist principle has taken more of a pummeling in recent years, but its truth cannot be surrendered. Indeed, this particular tenet shapes every doctrinal affirmation among Baptists. The ideas of voluntary faith, believer's baptism, hostility toward ecclesiastical hierarchy, and freedom of biblical interpretation—to mention only a few—all stem from this foundational profession of religious liberty.[4]

This belief has been particularly meaningful for me as I have struggled with traditionalist biblical hermeneutics in seeking to ascertain the role of women in church and home. Students often ask me how I became a feminist, wondering if being feminist is *really* compatible with being a Christian. I tell them it was by studying the life of Jesus and reading the epistles of Paul. Secular feminists such as Betty Friedan and Gloria Steinem pale in comparison to their radicality! Discovering that God does not issue calling or give gifts according to gender was a liberating insight. Perceiving that the subordination of women was theologically flawed (and not God's will!) allowed me to pursue with alacrity the beckoning of God to a nontraditional role in ministry.

Thankfully, I have been in good company; there have been a large number of men and women who have in the interest of freedom persevered in mining the biblical narratives.[5] Over the past two decades more and more Baptists have come to realize that their resistance to women's leadership in the church has little to do with scriptural prohibition and much to do with recalcitrant patriarchal views.

The fresh wind of the Spirit in Baptist life[6] today is evident in the influx of women serving on church staffs and the unprecedented number of women graduating from seminary and seeking pastorates. By God's grace and the new insight and receptivity of the congregations, many of these women are finding pastorates. More daunting, yet increasingly more common, is the emergence of women as church planters. Birthing new churches as an expression of their pastoral midwifery, these Baptists are constructing creative new patterns of Christian community. Many of us greet this move as a significant sign of ecclesial renewal; that is, the last barrier to full inclusion is being traversed.[7] In calling women as pastors, churches are finally living out the encompassing implications of our baptismal vows. "All are one in Christ Jesus"; therefore, the church much receive her daughters "for such a time as this." Religious liberty is alive among these Baptists.

I also remain Baptist because of the primacy of proclamation to all people. Baptists have followed the example of William Carey, who believed that we should both expect and attempt great things from and for God if we would be faithful in preaching the gospel. Last year I was privileged to offer the Belote Lectures at the Hong Kong Baptist Theological Seminary.[8] Prior to the lecture series I traveled in Macau and a southern province of China. Visiting churches, Bible Institutes, and one seminary, I encountered firsthand the missional efforts of generations of Baptists. Of course, other traditions had come to that part of the world, too; Anglican missionaries had made a great contribution in translation work and educating clergy. Yet, Baptists' unstinting work in the late 1900s and until the time of the cultural revolution continues to bear fruit to this day. After all, most Baptist groups place a high priority on missions.

Yet preaching the gospel has never been seen as enough; Baptists have tried to live it, too. "Following Jesus" has been the *sine qua non* of authentic discipleship. The tradition of the "social gospel" among Northern (now American) Baptists has been a favorite whipping boy of conservative critics. However, the expansive witness to the comprehensive claims of the gospel as seen in the writings of Walter Rauschenbusch is exemplary in fleshing out Baptist proclamation. His book *Christianity and the Social Crisis* (1907) thrust both him and this holistic perspective into national prominence. Often caricatured as a liberal, confident attempt to "build the kingdom," the social gospel movement nevertheless offered a needed corrective to those more concerned to "save souls" than to minister to the whole person. In many respects this movement presaged contemporary liberation theologies in its efforts to rectify the systemic evil that oppresses people.[9] This emphasis has been neglected in recent years as concerns about doctrinal heresy have preoccupied far too many Baptists.

There is a way to hold together the concern for right thinking *about* the faith and right acting *of* the faith. Healthy, flourishing churches keep the tension dynamic between orthodoxy and orthopraxy. Conviction and compassion can be mutually informative as we seek to follow Jesus in pragmatic ways.

Finally, I remain a persuaded Baptist because I believe it is a tradition open to reform. As Friedrich Schleiermacher put it, "The Reformation still goes on." We Baptists share in the insights of the left wing of the Reformation, the so-called radical reformers, whose ideas about baptism and discipleship got them roundly condemned. We also share in the theological breakthroughs about faith and scripture of the magisterial reformers, especially Luther and Calvin. The disparity between these two streams of reforming influence has been quite evident in recent years as scholars have attempted to illuminate the Baptist experience.[10]

The principle of *semper ecclesia reformanda* was established, but the tendency is to believe that theological insight is fixed and that all the difficult issues are resolved. The recent fragmentation among Baptists of the South, partially due to differing theological affirmations, suggests there is further work to be done as we move into the future.

I would suggest that contemporary Baptists need reform in several areas. First, we need liturgical renewal in our theology of the sacraments. Our adherence to Zwingli's "bare symbolism" has made our understanding of the Lord's Supper and baptism superficial. The Puritan influence, with its suspicion of liturgy (anything that might resemble Catholic or Anglican "ritual"), moved Eucharist to a negligible periphery in worship. It seems that Baptists have defined their theology of the "ordinances" more in reaction to others than in a constructive understanding of the graceful power of these "remembering signs."[11] Hence, baptism is little more than *imitatio Christi*, that is, we are to follow the example of our Lord Jesus Christ and submit to water baptism; we are to observe the Lord's Supper "in remembrance" as a memorial meal. This hardly begins to plumb the depths of the mystery of God's presence in this praxis of worship. Just as Moltmann has called the whole church to revisit the *filoque* clause that led to the schism of the Eastern and Western branches of Christianity over trinitarian theology, so must we look again at the delineations of sacramental theology in the disputes of our forebears that reformation might continue.

Another area currently being addressed in the interest of reform is the prominence of individualism among Baptists. While religious liberty, priesthood of the believer, and soul competence are rightly prized, they inexorably tend toward an individualistic expression of Baptist identity. I am encouraged by current attempts to revision Baptist identity as a communal, shared discipleship.[12] This is an important accentuation in a tradition marked more by personal experience than by corporate faith. The historic description of Baptists as the "gathered community" is enriching our ecclesiological understanding and practice.

More encouraging still is the new emphasis on spirituality that seeks to reclaim the common prereformation history of Christianity. Baptists are becoming acquainted with the ancient monastic disciplines of *lectio divina, oratio,* and *meditatio.* We are encountering the great teachers of prayer: Cyprian, Bernard of Clairvaux, Julian of Norwich, Francis of Assisi, and Teresa of Avila. We are even learning to call them "saints."[13]

Finally, I remain a Baptist because I still find this a constructive way of being Christian. I do not idolize our way as perfect, unsullied by political machinations and creedal missteps, but I cling to the vision of freedom in the context of responsibility that has shaped our common life. May we ever be reformed so as to live out our vocation in the body of Christ.

Notes

[1]I was ordained as a Southern Baptist minister in May 1983; in June 1997 I received Privilege of Call from American Baptist Churches, USA, which means having my ordination recognized.

[2]I must acknowledge my indebtedness to James Wm. McClendon, Jr., *Ethics: Systematic Theology*, vol. 1 (Nashville: Abingdon, 1986) 17-35, for his articulation of five distinctives of the "baptist vision": (1) biblicism, (2) mission, (3) liberty, (4) discipleship, and (5) community.

[3]I prefer believers' church to free church, although they are often used interchangeably. Believers' church focuses more on the attempt to live the Christian life as fully as possible while free church focuses more on a tradition of nonconformity. Both designations affirm the separation of church and state and a congregationalist church polity. For further interpretation of the origin of these terms, see *The Concept of the Believers' Church*, ed. James Leo Garrett, Jr. (Scottdale PA: Herald Press, 1969) and Thomas N. Finger, *Christian Theology: An Eschatological Approach*, vol. 2 (Scottdale PA: Herald Press, 1989) 236-40. Donald F. Durnbaugh's volume *The Believers' Church: The History and Character of Radical Protestantism* (New York: Macmillan, 1968), remains informative. See also the recent work of Miroslav Volf, *After Our Likeness: The Church as Image of the Trinity* (Grand Rapids: Eerdmans, 1998), for a sustained discussion of the significance of the free church tradition in larger ecumenical circles.

[4]James Wm. McClendon's project in constructive theology informed by the Baptist vision is very helpful in understanding the encompassing influence of the principle of religious liberty. See his *Ethics* (Nashville: Abingdon Press, 1986) and *Doctrine* (Nashville: Abingdon Press, 1994).

[5]One of the early texts that was extremely helpful to me was the study by Evelyn and Frank Stagg, *Women in the World of Jesus* (Philadelphia: Westminster Press, 1978). When I first read this, it was as if a whole new horizon opened before my eyes.

[6]Obviously here I am not referring to Southern Baptists, but to Cooperative Baptist Fellowship, the Alliance of Baptists, and American Baptist Churches.

[7]Nancy Hastings Sehested perceptively noted that while we can speak glibly about the priesthood of all believers (Baptists have no priests!), we are more than resistant to speaking of the "pastorhood of all believers." See her article "Women and Ministry in the Local Congregation," *Review and Expositor*, 83 (1986): 72.

[8]Recently, *Folio: A Newsletter for Baptist Women in Ministry* featured my recounting of this rich experience. See "Cultivating a Harvest of Sisters: Hong Kong Women in Ministry" (Winter 1998–1999).

[9]In my recent article, "The Changing Face of Baptist Discipleship," *Review and Expositor*, 95 (1998): 69, I refer to this form of discipleship as crusading or prophetic.

[10]See Paul Basden and David S. Dockery, eds., *The People of God: Essays on the Believers Church* (Nashville: Broadman Press, 1991); Robison B. James and David S. Dockery, eds., *Beyond the Impasse: Scripture, Interpretation, and Theology in Baptist Life* (Nashville: Broadman Press, 1992); and "Re-Envisioning Baptist Identity: A Manifesto for Baptist Communities in America," *Baptists Today*, 26 June 1997.

[11]This is McClendon's term in *Doctrine*, 386ff.

[12]See the so-called "Baptist Manifesto," *Baptists Today*, 26 June 1997, 8f.

[13]Jerry Moye has helpfully introduced Julian and Francis in his book *Praying with the Saints* (Macon GA: Peake Road, 1996).

A Baptist by Conviction
Emmanuel L. McCall, Sr.

Emmanuel L McCall

The Beginning

Like others, I grew up in a home where my mother, father, and grandmother were active in a local Baptist church. My adopted grandfather, who raised my orphaned father, was pastor of that church. I had church influence of the Baptist kind even from my birth, Rev. Samuel De Lane observed biblical traditions as closely as he could, so, following Old Testament tradition, on the eighth day I was dedicated and named Emmanuel Lemuel. At the dedication Rev. De Lane predicted that I would preach. The eight persons present were charged not to tell me of the prediction until its fulfillment. This came fourteen years later when I acknowledged God's call to me for His service.

Growing Up

Growing up in a home of dedicated Baptists, I learned Baptist perspectives. Our Pennsylvania church had dual membership in a National Baptist Convention and the American Baptist Convention. Literature and emphases from both conventions influenced our church life. The church was what I knew most. I was there for Sunday School, morning worship, and BYPU (Baptist Young People's Union and later BTU, or Baptist Training Union). Occasionally there were afternoon singings or interchurch visits. On Tuesday evenings I went with my parents to the Sunday School teachers meeting. On Thursday I went with my mother and grandmother to mission meetings and prayer service.

Kentucky Influence

When I began preaching, my pastor, Rev. Frank Waller, deeply instilled
Baptist doctrine and traditions. He was influenced by Dr. Marshall B.
Lanier, the premier theologian among National Baptists. Dr. Lanier
served Simmons University (now Simmons Bible College) in Louisville, Kentucky, as dean, teacher, and president from 1915 to 1961. He
taught actively until his death at age 96. Lanier's theology was greatly
influenced by W. T. Conner of Southwestern Baptist Theological Seminary and Augustus Hopkins Strong. Lanier was most responsible for
the theological direction of older black Baptists, since he regularly
taught at the National Baptist Convention's training events and taught
the many ministers who passed through Simmons.

Academic Mentor

It was this influence that caused Rev. Waller to insist that I go to
Simmons for theological training. After arriving at Simmons, immediately out of high school, I was counseled by Dr. Garland K. Offutt, a
prominent pastor and faculty member. Dr. Offutt was the first African-
American to graduate from the Southern Baptist Theological Seminary
(M.Th. 1946, Th.D. 1949). Offutt helped me to understand the proper
procedures for obtaining an adequate theological education. Because
Simmons was then an institute, he suggested I get my college training
and later go to Southern. That became my plan, but since I lacked the
money necessary for college, I remained at Simmons for a year. I
received the impress of Dr. Lanier and the Simmons tradition.

That also became a time when I seriously began examining what I
was hearing. Lanier was heavily influenced by Calvinistic theology. He
had been a Presbyterian pastor until the invitation to join the Simmons
University faculty.

My classmates were all older men. I was warned not to ask questions or challenge what I heard. My inquisitive mind would not allow
me to remain silent, however. Some of what I was hearing seemed worthy of challenge. I remembered having heard from BTU that Baptists
had freedom of conscience and the availability of the Holy Spirit to
teach each of us. I had heard about "soul competency" as a hallmark of
Baptist tradition. I had been encouraged to think for myself. I found it

difficult to remain docile to anything unexplained, illogical, or even irrational. This didn't set well with my classmates, who appeared more eager for an infusion of what they were told to believe, even if they did not clearly understand it.

A New Family

In the fall of 1954 I began studies at the University of Louisville (U of L). Several things assisted my intellectual and spiritual quest. The curricula taught me how to think and utilize the resources available, and I was blessed to be part of a nurturing spiritual and social family known as the Baptist Student Union (BSU). The BSU director, Fred Witty, and two students visited in my dorm room following registration. They noted that I had filled out "Baptist Preference" on the religious activity card. They invited me to the BSU. The programs challenged my intellectual and spiritual growth. We often heard from Southern Seminary profs and students, in addition to local pastors.

My BSU family became my strength during my college years. It was my BSU family that helped me challenge the racism of the U of L community environment, and even in the Long Run Baptist Association. A delegation of pastors was sent to direct the BSU not to allow non-Southern Baptists to participate in its programs. American Baptist students from across the Ohio River in Indiana and four of us who were black were particularly affected. My BSU family challenged and defied the status quo. This challenge even extended to state and national student events. Indelibly etched in my mind was the bus trip to Student Week at Ridgecrest Baptist Assembly in 1957. Somewhere in Tennessee we stopped at a bus terminal. It was assumed to be a place where non-whites could eat. When the two Chinese and Indian students and I were told to get out of the cafeteria line, it was my Baptist family that protested by walking out en masse, even though some had not paid for their meals. At Ridgecrest my Baptist family saw to it that I felt affirmed and accepted in what was the beginning of a changing and volatile era.

A Challenge to Baptist Identity

Perhaps the greatest challenge to my Baptist identity came during my college years. Members of the African Methodist denominations, Lutherans, Episcopals, and Presbyterians often recruited me to preach. They were looking for potential pastors whom they could prepare for their churches. Each church offered a full scholarship if I would make the switch. Even though I had to work eight hours each day after class, cramming study in when I could, my Baptist heritage and Baptist family were too precious for me to forsake. My roots were firmly planted.

The recruiters were dumbfounded at how I could remain Baptist, given their perception of "Baptist anti-intellectualism" and the racism then evident in the Southern Baptist Convention. For me, this was no problem. Both my heritage and experience had introduced me to Baptist intellectuals. My National Baptist upbringing had introduced me to "giants of the mind." I also had the love and affirmation of my BSU family and the budding relationships at Southern Seminary. This I could not and would not forsake.

For the last twenty-one years I have served on the board of trustees of the Interdenominational Theological Seminary in Atlanta. I have often appreciated our Baptist heritage as I have seen those from other denominations moved around, sometimes against their will, or at the capriciousness of presiding bishops.

Doctoral study at Emory University also helped me to appreciate my Baptist heritage. While my fellow students were grappling with basic scriptural truths, my Baptist heritage had equipped me to move confidently in areas yet to be explored. Learning more about other denominations and their traditions helped me to understand my Baptist heritage. I came out of the experience confirmed in the substance of my faith.

✝✝✝✝

After fifty-seven years as a Christian and forty-eight years as a proclaimer of God's Word, I can say "I am a Baptist by conviction." We Baptists have our problems and shortcomings. We have areas where we need to grow. But for as long as the Lord lets me live, I want to participate in our challenge of proclaiming the lordship of Jesus Christ.

The Four "C"s of Being Baptist

— *Gary Parker* —

Gary E. Parker

A couple of years ago I attended a dinner at which Will Campbell, a Baptist prophet whose sword cuts on both sides, received an award for his ongoing courage as a writer and spokesperson for religious freedom. Michael Clingenpeel, editor of the *Religious Herald* of Virginia, introduced Campbell. In that introduction Clingenpeel told this story. Since Campbell didn't refute the story when he stood up to receive his award, I assume it is true.

Campbell found himself in an airport one day about to go through the scanning device at the security checkpoint. The security guard asked Campbell to give him his cane (Campbell uses one these days to help him get around) so he could run it through the x-ray machine.

"But I need my cane to walk," said Campbell.

"I'm sorry, but I have to run it through the x-ray," insisted the guard.

"But I have a bad leg," continued Campbell.

"I have to inspect the cane," said the guard, sticking to the rules like gum to a shoe bottom.

Campbell turned to his wife who waited patiently at his side. "Do I look like a terrorist?" he asked her.

"No, but that doesn't matter," she said, "Give the man your cane. He's just doing his job."

By that time a multitude of people had lined up like boxcars to a freight train behind the irascible Campbell. On tiptoes the people leaned forward, eyes wide and ears pricked in an effort to see what the commotion was about.

With a shrug of dismissal, Campbell handed his cane to the guard. But then, instead of walking through the checkpoint, he dropped to his knees, stretched out full-length on the floor and crawled like a snake through the security zone—elbow to ground, knee following elbow, elbow then knee, elbow then knee, ever so slowly he made his way past the startled guard.

Finally, when he reached the other side, Campbell pulled himself to his feet, took his cane from the red-faced security man, and walked away. Halfway down the corridor, Campbell's dear but mortified wife leaned close to him and said, "Honey, why in the world do you do things like that?"

To which Campbell replied, "Because I'm a Baptist, that's why!"

I love the Campbell story for one simple reason: it shows me a man who apparently likes being a Baptist and knows why he likes it. To Campbell, living as a Baptist gives him a radical kind of freedom to say and do what he believes. He knows why he is what he is. I think that's a valuable lesson for all of us—to know why we are what we are.

In this essay I'm supposed to describe why I'm a Baptist. Obviously, that question relates directly to me as an individual. At the same time, though, it also relates to the broader body of believers who wear the Baptist label. Why is anyone a Baptist? What leads someone to live out their Christian faith in this particular expression of the body of Christ?

Though we don't like to admit it, I suspect that many people who attend a local "Baptist" church and accept that tag on their brand of faith do so without having any real sense of why. I know that statement carries a word of judgment in it. Yet, as I observe the Baptist landscape (through fifteen years as a pastor and three as a "Coordinator of Baptist Principles"), I think it's true—at least it was for many years in my own Christian experience. As I survey the scene, it seems that people come into "Baptistness" through three particular doors of entry.

Baptist by Conception

Three years ago my family and I moved to Atlanta, Georgia. My wife Melody, who had lived her entire life as either a preacher's kid or a preacher's wife, decided she wanted to visit a Presbyterian Church (just for the heck of it, she said) before we settled down as members of a Baptist congregation. So, one Sunday morning when I was out of town, she woke up, dressed, and told our two daughters of her plans. But guess what? My seven-year-old, Ashley, refused. "We can't go to a Presbyterian church!" she declared (as if holding the line against Melody's obvious blasphemy). "We're Baptists!"

Did Ashley know what being Baptist meant? Not particularly. But she demonstrated something important to admit. Many of us are Baptist because we are born into it. We get dedicated in a Baptist church when we're infants; we get "dunked" in Baptist waters when we make a profession of faith; we eat covered-dish dinners under the trees in the back and go on ski retreats with our friends and sing ten thousand stanzas of "Just As I Am" before we're eighteen. We breathe Baptist air and drink Baptist water and eat Baptist chicken. All of this is valuable and good, but it may not be complete.

No doubt you've heard the statement "Baptist born and Baptist bred, and when I'm gone I'll be Baptist dead." Now, the reality is that you can't really be "Baptist born" (since Baptists don't practice infant baptism), but I still like that statement because it speaks of a lifelong loyalty to a particular view of faith. But let's also understand the downside of this concept. Being Baptist because of the chance circumstance of our birth says nothing about any kind of genuine commitment to authentic Baptist convictions. It is true that those convictions may become ingrained in us by a lifetime of Baptist "osmosis," but not necessarily so. If we are not diligent, we will allow that which we have always known to keep us from determining that which we truly believe.

Baptist by Connection

I became a Christian at the age of eighteen and immediately joined the Coronaca Baptist Church outside of Greenwood, South Carolina, and received baptism. To the people in that church, I was a Baptist from that moment forward. But why did I join that particular version of the Christian community? Was it because I knew and understood the beliefs championed by Roger Williams, John Leland, Ann Judson, George Truett, and Cecil Sherman? Not at all. I joined Coronaca because the girl I dated at the time was a member of that church, and I

wanted to attend with her. My connection with another person
ushered me into that church.

You know how that works: you marry a Baptist and so become
one; you live near a Baptist church and attend it because it is so con-
venient; a neighbor asks you to attend a concert at a Baptist church
during Advent, and you go and never stop going. I applaud all of these
connections and see them as God-given, but if our understanding of
our faith tradition goes no further, we lose the rich texture of a history
and belief system that merits our examination.

Baptist by Conviction

Even as we accept the value of the various doors into Baptistness, I suggest a third and, in my way of thinking, better reason, for living faith as
a Baptist. It seems to me that to become truly Baptist means we move
beyond "Baptist by conception" and "Baptist by connection." To be
authentically Baptist is to become a Baptist by conviction. By this I
mean we examine the core beliefs of our faith family and measure
them by what we believe to be biblically sound and historically true.

In my own case this didn't happen until I left my hometown and
entered college. At Anderson College and Furman University I came
into contact with scores of people of other faith traditions. I attended
churches of all kinds—Catholic, Episcopalian, Methodist. I even dated
a Jewish co-ed for a short time and ventured to her synagogue.
Although I didn't recognize it at the time, those experiences during
college were part of a sifting process for me—a time to compare and
contrast, accept and reject, adopt and jettison. By the time I matricu-
lated to seminary, I knew a great deal more about the core convictions
that had birthed and sustained the religious family I had decided to call
my own. Even more importantly, I had internalized those convictions
and found that they resonated with my understanding of biblical faith.

You know these convictions as well or better than I, but I will state
them briefly for the sake of review. Historically, Baptists have staked
their denominational tent on these five pegs:

• *Believer's Baptism*—Each person must come to a conscious commitment to Jesus Christ before he/she wades into the waters of baptism.

- *Priesthood of the Believer*—Each person has direct access to God without the necessity of a human intermediary (pope, priest, pastor, or civil magistrate); the priesthood allows the freedom of personal belief and the responsibility of personal service to others in the Christian community.

- *Autonomy of the Local Church*—Every congregation has the right to decide whom it will ordain, how it will conduct its ordinances, where it will spend its money, who will serve as its ministers, and how it will relate to the larger body of Baptists and other Christians.

- *Separation of Church and State*—The state should not coerce anyone into any religious belief, specific or general; the church should neither expect nor accept any government interference in the advancement of religion, even if that religion happens to be the individual choice on the buffet line of options.

- *Confessional but not Creedal Commitment to the Bible*—Confessions describe the Baptist understanding of the Bible's teachings, but reject any attempt to impose a creed over and above the Bible as a barometer of faith and orthodoxy.

The bottom line is, I like to think I'm a Baptist because of my commitment to these principles. I believe in what they symbolize—the freedom and responsibility to take my own relationship to God seriously; to study the Scriptures and apply them to my life without dictate from some "higher human" authority; to serve in a local church with the understanding that my church is fully the body of Christ in its own individual setting; to live as a citizen of a nation in which religion is always let loose but is never propped up. The truth is, I'm a Baptist because these principles have become a part of my inner core, my conscience.

Baptist by Conscience

Perhaps I have it all wrong here, and someone will surely correct me if I do, but it seems to me that we who are Baptists ultimately need to take this final step. We need the passion of our consciences to warm our distinctive beliefs. Otherwise we may offer to others the bread of who we are and what we believe, but they will taste it and find it cold on their tongues. Passion may make some nervous, but cold reason makes few converts.

When I think of Roger Williams, I think of a man driven by what he felt *and* what he believed. When I think of Martin Luther King, Jr., I think of a man of thunder *and* of intellect. When I think of Ann Judson, I think of a woman of zeal *and* of compassion. When I think of Will Campbell, I think of a man with fire in his bones *and* precision in his speech.

Why am I a Baptist? Originally, because of a connection to a brown-eyed brunette from Greenwood, South Carolina. Later, because of an understanding of authentic Baptist beliefs. And now, because these beliefs have risen up and taken on blood and bone and sinew as part of who I am. It may be true that I am not always a good Baptist, but never let it be said that I am a dispassionate one.

Gratefully Baptist

—— *R. Keith Parks* ——

"I am an old ignorant woman, and I don't understand many things, but I do understand about believing in Jesus." Minah was giving her testimony, required of candidates for baptism at Iman Baptist Church in Semarang, Indonesia. At age forty-six she was considered old, because Indonesians' average life expectancy at the time was less than thirty years. And though she was illiterate, she was not ignorant.

I found myself thinking that since she did not read and since I had been her teacher in the new Christians' class, everything she knew about being a Christian depended upon me. I was praying that I had taught her correctly and covered all the bases and that neither she nor I would be embarrassed by her testimony. But I had forgotten what it means to be a Baptist kind of Christian.

Minah repeated, "Although I don't understand many things, I do understand about being a Christian." She looked at my wife, Helen Jean, and me for support, and then she continued. You could sense she was trying to explain what is beyond explanation. And then she added, "Why, it is just like Jesus was down inside my heart explaining these things to me."

She sat down, the congregation voted to baptize her, and I relearned a significant lesson: I was not her real teacher. As Jesus promised, the Holy Spirit had taught her and was continuing to teach her.

Minah's testimony reminded me that Baptists believe when persons trust Christ, his Spirit interacts directly with them, and they are not dependent on anyone else as a go-between. In choosing to trust Jesus Christ as one's personal Savior, a person is born into the family of

God and becomes a member of the body of Christ. The experience cannot be taught by a missionary or learned in a catechism. It occurs only in a personal encounter with the living Christ and a deliberate choice to follow him.

At that worship service in Indonesia, I felt the power of personal testimony and the encouragement it gives to members of a local church. I sensed the congregation's enthusiasm as they received Minah into that local body and affirmed her baptism as a declaration to the world. It was a Baptist moment.

I am Baptist because we understand the New Testament to teach that individuals, when able to decide between right and wrong, must make a personal choice to accept Christ as his or her Savior. When this occurs, the Holy Spirit does in fact come to live in that person and is his or her spiritual teacher.

The New Testament, however, does not stop with individual conversion. Inevitably the Holy Spirit links that individual with a fellowship of believers. I have the conviction that the conversion experience has built into it an innate need and desire to link life and spirit with others in order to worship and serve the Lord Jesus.

Whereas I believe that all authentic Christians are part of the "universal church," as referenced in Paul's letter to the Ephesians, I am equally convinced that the local church has unique significance. In fact, the vast majority of references to *eklesia* ("the church" or "called-out-ones") in the New Testament is to the local gathering of Christians.

This miracle organism is the group through which Christ has promised to work out on earth what has been determined in heaven. This group becomes authentic because a Christ-breathed fellowship (*koinonia*) unites them to Christ and to each other. This the only thing that can truly forge a widely diverse group of individuals into a local fellowship (church). Having one's name on a church roll, believing certain doctrines, or participating in worship or activities does not create a true church. Oneness with each other in Christ does!

One of the greatest illustrations of this concept comes from working with Indonesian seminary students in an outreach project in Central Java. Those young believers, armed only with a New Testament in their hands and the Holy Spirit in their hearts, went into small towns and villages where the gospel had not been preached. We tried not to impose any American cultural expression on their Christian faith. In that setting, with no corrupted models of churches, it was refreshing to see what happened. We stood in awe as "church" happened. We watched as those converted inevitably worshiped together, relied on Scripture, and accepted responsibility as a new fellowship of believers. They banded together to reach out to others. They quietly resisted the inevitable criticism and pressures from the majority religion and from government control. They practiced those distinctives that we as Baptists have declared through the years to be ours:

- conversion of persons who reach the age of accountability and baptism of believers only

- priesthood of every believer

- autonomy of local congregations

- all beliefs and practice based on the Bible

- separation of church and state

- associational principle: autonomous churches choose to cooperate to reach the world in a way none can do alone

The first four distinctives are held by most Baptists. The fifth is a common belief among Baptists in America. The sixth is the added concept that formed the Southern Baptist Convention in 1845. The only significant action of that first convention was to establish a Board of Foreign Missions and a Board of Domestic Missions. That simple but grand vision was powerful enough to make autonomous churches choose to give up some of their independence for the greater good of extending the Kingdom of God throughout the earth. It was biblical and unifying.

None of our distinctives are held by Baptists alone. Yet the unique combination creates a different kind of Christian group. It defines the heritage of authentic Southern Baptists. Each principle is essential. Any substitution radically changes the nature of what Southern Baptists have believed. These six basic beliefs are woven together and are so interdependent that to remove any one of the threads is to unravel the whole Baptist cloth.

The six beliefs are spiritually joined to each other. The health of the body requires all of them in relationship. The priesthood of each believer is an outgrowth of the basic experience of personal regeneration. Everyone who comes into a personal relationship with Jesus Christ has direct access to God and God's Word through the Holy Spirit.

As believers come together in a church, each one is to submit his or her spiritual relationship voluntarily to the combined spiritual understanding of all the members. The New Testament teaches that spiritual wisdom channeled through the local group provides more mature understanding. Each group is accountable directly to God and only to God. How can any outside individual or group be in a position to understand God's leadership for that local group?

The marvel of Southern Baptists is that independent individuals submit to autonomous churches, and that in turn, these autonomous churches freely give what no one has authority to take. Churches surrender a portion of their independence to achieve the extension of the Kingdom of God.

This Kingdom extension, usually referred to as the joint mission effort of cooperating churches, is challenging enough to combine the prayers, finances, and lives of missionaries of all involved churches. No other cohesive force has ever held Baptists or any other group together in such numbers with such results.

Historically, *other* Baptists have come together around doctrine. Inevitably they have divided as they disagreed about interpretations of scripture or correct doctrine. Current Southern Baptist leadership is moving down this path. Not only does this trend reject *Southern* Baptist heritage, but also it leads to fragmentation.

Baptists who hold traditional biblical convictions inevitably reject state control of religion along with religious control of the state. This is the scriptural principle based on "rendering to Caesar what belongs to Caesar . . . and to God what belongs to God"(Matt 22:21) and obeying God rather than humans (Acts 4:19-20). But it is also an inescapable conclusion of genuine Baptists that their source of authority is different. No authority, neither religious nor civil, can intervene. Genuine Baptists act on the basis of cooperation. The state must coerce. There is absolutely no basis for either controlling the other.

Southern Baptists have traditionally been *confessional*, not *creedal* Christians. Confessional Christians invite others who are in agreement to join their group. Creedal Christians define exact beliefs and determine whether or not others are acceptable to join their group. In the confessional approach those who join determine whether they agree and want to join. In the creedal approach the keepers of the creed determine who qualifies to join.

In recent years an increasing number of individuals have said to me what a Southern Baptist friend declared: "I am no longer a Southern Baptist." A committed Christian and longtime Bible teacher in her local church, she actually was expressing extreme disagreement with pronouncements, attitudes, and actions of national Southern Baptist Convention leaders. "Aren't you still a member of _____ Baptist Church?" I asked rhetorically. "Don't you still hold basic Baptist beliefs?" I agree with her analysis of the damage done to our Christian witness by the hostile takeover of the Convention, but I reached a different conclusion. "Certainly you are still a Southern Baptist," I maintained. "Relating to the state Baptist convention is not what makes you Southern Baptist! Relating to the national convention is not what makes you Southern Baptist! Personally believing Baptist distinctives and being a member of a local Southern Baptist church is what makes you Southern Baptist!"

I personally am still a Southern Baptist because I hold Baptist convictions and am a member of a Southern Baptist church. But our denomination has changed. Current national leaders are eroding Baptist principles such as priesthood of the believer, autonomy of the local church, and separation of church and state. They are moving from a confessional Baptist approach to a creedal one. They are trying to substitute doctrine for missions as the Convention's cohesive force.

Current trends in society and changes in culture would have eroded the convention model eventually. Regrettably, the controversy has speeded up this process. Not only has there been a great loss in the change of structure, but also the very essence of being Baptist has been radically altered.

Yet the heritage of Southern Baptists is being lived out now, I believe, in the Cooperative Baptist Fellowship. That is why I am a part of CBF. Once again Baptists are joined together around missions. Our historic Baptist principles are valued and practiced. There is hope for a real Baptist future.

I am Baptist, nurtured as a Southern Baptist and continuing those beliefs and practices as part of CBF. I have found biblical, spiritual freedom among these "free and faithful" Baptists.

I am Baptist because of the conviction that our distinctives are biblical. Although I was guided and shaped by an honest cattle-trader father and a wise, loving mother, no person or group of persons caused me to become Baptist. I was influenced and challenged in churches, in the Baptist Student Union on a state campus, and in seminary. The theories I learned in those settings were refined and strengthened while I was a pastor and a missionary. They have been nurtured by missionaries, work colleagues, and Christian friends of the world—Baptist and others.

Just as no group made me Baptist, no group can coerce me to surrender my heritage of convictions. Certainly there are other authentic expressions of Christianity, but I am grateful mine is Baptist.

An Invitational People
A Relational Response

James M. Pitts

An invitation in a Baptist setting is understood as an evangelistic appeal at the end of a sermon. At the conclusion of most Baptist worship services, especially in revival services, an invitation is given. The "doors of the church" are open. The congregation sings countless verses of "Just As I Am." Extending an invitation sometimes means that it is literally drawn out. With every head bowed and every eye closed, the choir provides a choral background for the preacher's passionate plea. "This is the hour of decision! This is the sacred moment of response. Now is the time for a personal and public commitment to Christ and the church."

Walking the aisle, being welcomed by the pastor, expressing your intentions, filling out a decision card with your name and address, being presented to the congregation: all these form the revered ritual of invitation. This sacred ceremony is the highlight and climax of worship.

As a Baptist, I am grateful that we are an invitational people. However, by invitation I mean something much more than a song. Baptists, at our best, have a spirit of acceptance and affirmation. In my pilgrimage of faith I was not persuaded by powerful preaching, emotionally moved by a gospel song, or awed by a spectacle in an arena. People, not celebrities but ordinary persons who genuinely loved God and liked people, touched me.

In a busy world filled with more "important" things to do, these ordinary persons became special. They took time to let me know that they really cared for me. They took time to know my name and me. They conveyed that I was someone who mattered, not only in God's eyes, but also in theirs. My hopes and dreams, fears and failures were really important to them. In their homes and classrooms, church doorways and youth groups, they faithfully communicated that I was somebody. I was a person who was valuable and capable, worthy of their respect and trust, filled with potential and promise. These people were busy and successful, but even more than success they valued faith, hope, love, and me.

Each of us is unique. My situation in life was out of the ordinary. My parental family would not be chosen for the cover of a Christian family magazine. Born in Washington, D.C., in many ways I was privileged. I was exposed early to racial and ethnic diversity, religious pluralism, and an exceptional educational environment. Our nation's capital city is filled with museums, galleries, and libraries. The National Zoo was my afternoon playground. The Smithsonian Museums and the Washington Mall were my Saturday excursions. The Corcoran School of Art was my adolescent passion. Yet on the home front, despite our middle class affluence, there was an emotional and spiritual vacuum.

My parents, both successful professionals, were unable to live together. My need for harmony and security at home was overshadowed by my mother's inability to control her drinking. The nation was engaged in World War II. Matching the air-raid blackouts with drawn window shades and sirens, the drapes on our windows hid from public view scenes of domestic violence, alcohol blackouts, and muffled screams of conflict. It was a suffocating atmosphere of repetitive crises creating a numbing lethargy to life.

Sensitive to our dysfunctional plight, a kindly and caring Baptist pastor attempted to intervene and offer guidance. His well-meaning invitation was rejected. In my mother's confused search for stability she explored a wide range of options from failed attempts at suicide to eclectic spirituality. One quest involved her momentary embrace of the Baha'i religion and placing me as a resident in a nearby Baha'i boarding school.

Unfortunately, nothing was able to stop the downward spiral and disintegration of my parents' marriage. To rescue the children from this whirlpool of addiction and pain, my father accepted his mother's invitation to provide refuge and hospitality for my brother and me. Her generous offer was a sheer gift of grace. Grandmother was widowed at the age of forty-four. Single-handed, with God's help and disciplined perseverance, she raised ten children.

I did not realize it at the time, but she was establishing a foundation for faith. She cared for us, loved and disciplined us, laughed and cried with us, and nursed me through chicken pox and my younger brother through diphtheria. She read the Bible to us, taught us to pray, and took us to church. She became a living reminder of God's love and presence. Through her life and witness we were introduced to Jesus, the redeeming and reconciling Lord who strengthened and sustained her. And as you have probably concluded, yes, Grandmother was a Baptist.

I had years and miles to go before being a Baptist was my personal choice, but my identity as a Baptist Christian had been established. There was no pressure from Grandmother or her congregational family, but a willingness to wait in faith and with hope. They were willing to wait on my increasing maturity and ability to make a personal decision regarding a public affirmation of faith, baptism, and church membership.

Faith is caught more than it is taught. Entrance into the believing community is an invitational process into which we are spiritually birthed, nurtured, and matured as generative members. Baptists at their best are not anxious or angry. They are people who have freely joined together to worship and witness, nurture and educate, comfort and encourage. They begin locally and form partnerships globally to follow the Great Commission to preach, teach, and heal in Jesus' name.

Because often we are a minority, Baptists are empathetic to religious minorities and supportive of religious freedom for all. Traditionally we affirm openness to truth, respect for individuals, and religious freedom. Baptists are not the protectors and keepers of the dominant culture, the hall monitors of society, the moral managers of the larger culture, or the self-appointed defenders of any political establishment. Baptists have intentionally rejected the powerful centers of privilege. We are comfortable on the margins of societal structures, offering a prophetic witness, pleading the cause of the disenfranchised and victims of injustice. Life on the margins is both freeing and challenging as we live on the cutting edge of change.

The litmus test for a healthy congregation of Baptists, in touch with the Lord and our free church heritage, is that we are filled with faith and freedom, humility and honesty, affirmation and praise. When Baptists become dysfunctional, like a family living with a drunk, they are filled with discord regarding power and control, conflictive and complaining. Sick religion promotes uproar and division, fear and distrust.

Baptists generally have been ordinary people, not the ruling elite, powerful establishment types, but hard-working common folk, and primarily poor. Within the Baptist fellowship persons from all walks of life have found a gracious acceptance and experienced a personal affirmation that transcends culture and class. The simplicity of the gospel was good news they were hungry to hear. Hearts have been touched and lives inspired by a dynamic faith not subordinated to rules of rigid conformity and dogmatic creedalism.

My childhood interlude with my paternal grandmother forever shaped my relationship with others, myself, and God. During my middle school years my father remarried. My stepmother was from a high church tradition. Our new home was adjacent to that tall steeple edifice. With its geographical proximity and the welcome of the vicar, I found a place in its youth activities. Parish life and public worship were done truly by the book. The service book, with its tried and true rules and regulations, was not to be changed. A perception of nonnegotiable, unwavering religious authority, especially by a turbulent teenager, is always problematic.

The flash point of conflict centered on an invitational moment. As a church youth group officer, I suggested that we sponsor the showing of a Billy Graham evangelistic film. My proposal was accepted. A Sunday evening date was scheduled. Thanks to promotion and prayer, a number of persons from the congregation and the community came out to see the film. At its conclusion a representative of the Billy Graham organization offered an invitation for anyone to come forward who wanted to make a public profession of his or her faith. A hymn was sung, but no one responded. A closing prayer was pronounced, and the service was over.

Following the service the buzz among the youth and congregation was one of dismay. The concern was not that no one had responded, but that the representative had assumed someone present was not a believer. A public invitation, from their perspective, was totally out of character with the way they went about being and doing church. They thought it was presumptuous, arrogant, rude, and simply in bad taste. That incident threw my spiritual and relational life into turmoil. Then I remembered my early childhood interlude with Grandmother and Baptists.

Twelve blocks north of our high-rise apartment was a Baptist church. It was the same congregation whose pastor had reached out and was rejected by my parents in their hour of need. As a high school senior, I showed up at the door of that church. I knew no one, other than the pastor who had impressed me when I was a child as someone who loved God and liked people. His home was a block away from where we had lived earlier. As a youngster, he responded to my request and loaned me his family's dog so that I could take a pet to school for "show and tell."

At the front door of the church Miss Mamie Davis and Mr. Clifton Mack welcomed me. They made me believe that I was somebody, a person of importance. They called me by name. They acted like they genuinely cared for me. They were glad I was present. They welcomed me as if I were family.

The youth group was dynamic and challenging both to my head and my heart. Harold Stassen, former governor of Minnesota and a member of the U.S. President's cabinet, was an active leader in the church. He was present not only on Sunday, but also drove his old station wagon to midweek services. His son, Glen, then a college student at the University of Virginia (now a professor at Fuller Theological Seminary), became a mentor and model. Full of freshman philosophy, Glen had questions for the youth to ponder concerning God, the vastness of space, the purpose of life, and the meaning of time. The pastor, Edward O. Clark, was a student of Walter Rauschenbush and a friend of Clarence Jordan.

Affiliated with the local Baptist association, the Washington Coun-cil of Churches, the American Baptist Convention, and the Southern Baptist Convention, the Chevy Chase congregation was not a franchise controlled by outside hierarchical power. The members had the audacity to believe they were competent as believers to interpret the Scriptures rightly under the guidance of the Holy Spirit, to be the church and to do the work of Christ in the world. They believed the church should be composed of regenerate persons who freely chose to embrace faith and follow the Christ. Baptism was for believers who personally and voluntarily chose to follow Christ. The way of faith into full membership was through "believer's baptism," which for them was represented at its biblical best through immersion.

Worship in that family of faith was not a media event, a fine arts concert, or a "meeting house in Dixie" shouting service. It was not "a light and sound" arena show featuring strutting exhibitionist stars with color-coded microphones. The sanctuary was a place of heartfelt rever-ence. There I experienced worship that was responsive to the finest aspirations and gifts of the congregation. The sermons interpreted scripture and connected with daily life. Music and prayers, the Lord's Supper and baptism, weddings and funerals all communicated an inviting and ecumenical spirit.

I wondered how a Billy Graham film would play within this con-gregation. I talked it up to various folks—youth, adults, the pastor. All were receptive. Contacts were made. A day and date were scheduled. Same film, same Billy Graham representative, same neighborhood; only the congregation was different. On the Sunday evening of the film's showing the sanctuary was filled. At the conclusion of the film an invitation was extended. During the singing of the hymn several people responded, making a profession of faith or rededicating themselves to the way and cause of Christ. During that service I felt a sense of spiritual fulfillment and a confirmation of my own calling to ministry.

As a seventeen-year-old, little did I know what would be involved on the road ahead. But there was a sense of excitement, wonder, and awe. And in a real sense, I knew that I had found home. I had found a family, an extended family of faith. What was personal had become public. What I experienced as local, later I would realize is global. The folks who invited and embraced me, accepted and affirmed me, were not confined to a particular geographical region.

Baptists comprise a fellowship of 188 unions and conventions with a membership of more than 41 million baptized believers. Together the Baptist community embraces an extended family of approximately 100 million persons in more than 200 countries. We are involved in missions, education, defending human rights, and responding to social and spiritual needs.

Baptists are a diverse fellowship. We claim as part of our legacy John Bunyan, Roger Williams, Lottie Moon, Walter Rauschenbush, Harry Emerson Fosdick, Clarence and Florence Jordan, and Martin and Mabel England. Today the roll call of Baptists includes Strom Thurman and Bill Clinton, Martin Luther King and Jesse Jackson, Jesse Helms and Jimmy Carter, Millard Fuller and Tony Campolo.

Historically, we identify John Smyth and Thomas Helwys as two of the first English-speaking Baptists. Perhaps one of the reasons for the confused identity of contemporary Baptists, especially here in the United States, is that we have ignored our left-wing English Reformation roots. Lutherans with Martin Luther, Presbyterians with John Calvin, or Methodists with John and Charles Wesley, all have created larger-than-life icons of mythic proportions. These historic personalities convey the distinctive characteristics of their denominational heritages.

By and large, during the last half of the twentieth century we Baptists have failed in our attempts to communicate and personalize our religious heritage. Mention Smyth and Helwys, and many think you are speaking of Smith & Wesson, a firearms manufacturer. The history of English Baptists began with a group of religious refugees in Holland, led by John Smyth, a former Anglican priest, and Thomas Helwys, a country gentleman who had been educated in law. About 1611 or 1612 Thomas Helwys and a handful of followers returned to English soil.

That little band of believers returned to the country where they had been persecuted in order to propagate their faith. The Baptist witness was established and perpetuated by ten courageous persons, who established the first Baptist church on English soil at Spitalfield, just outside the walls of London. They believed that Christ died for all people and that the church should be composed of regenerate persons. They believed in liberty of conscience and made the first claim for religious freedom to be published in the English language. For his witness, Helwys was imprisoned and a few years later died.

Following Thomas Helwys, leadership of the Spitalfield congregation was taken over by John Murton. He continued the plea for religious liberty, writing that "no man ought to be persecuted for his religion." The primary concern of Baptists was religious freedom, a faith that is personal and voluntary. They affirmed the centrality of the individual, the primacy of the personal, conversion by conviction, and baptism for believers. It was this kind of freedom that lured religious nonconformists to America.

The best of the Baptist heritage comprises a classic tradition of men and women who love God and like people and who affirm the God-given freedom of all people. I am talking about free and faithful Baptist believers who are free to read, study, and interpret the Bible for themselves.

We are free to deal with God without the imposition of creed or the interference of clergy or government. We are free to order our worship and work as a congregation under the lordship of Christ. We are free to ordain persons we perceive as gifted for ministry. We are free to voluntarily participate in the unity and mission of Christ.

We promote religious freedom for all. This means that all persons are free to have religion or to abstain from religion. Classic, old-fashioned Baptists always have known the difference between Christ and Caesar. We know that to blend the power of the state with the church pollutes the cause of Christ and denies the freedom God gives to all.

Why am I a Baptist? First, I accepted the invitation to be a Christian. What initially brings Baptist Christians together is an invitation to accept Jesus as Savior and to follow Christ as our Lord. Second, I made a relational response and embraced the fellowship of believers that invited and accepted me. I freely chose to accept their invitation to be a part of an ongoing, racially diverse, culturally pluralistic fellowship committed to religious freedom.

Baptists at their best are filled with faith and freedom, humility and honesty, affirmation and praise. It is my hope and prayer that this will be your experience.

Baptist Debts, Baptist Doubts

——— *Charles E. Poole* ———

I don't think I've ever seen five words resist getting in line as fiercely as have the five assigned to me. I carefully arrange them in order so that they form into the assigned topic, "Why I Am a Baptist." But the second I turn my head, "Am" and "I" get out of line, swap places, and form a question. I'm going to try one more time to write those five words and make them stay in order. Here goes: "Why Am I a Baptist?"

You see what I mean. I can't quite make it come out as a declaration. Hand me those five words to work with, and I can't make them behave. They insist on getting out of line. I think they must know that in my pen, on my paper, from my heart, they are probably arranged more honestly as a wondering question than as an enthusiastic affirmation.

I do wonder. Not much, or often, do I wonder. I can go long seasons without giving it much thought. But the invitation to write these words has painted me back into an old corner where I have to wonder again, out loud, "Why, after all, am I a Baptist?"

The fact that I wonder why I'm still a Baptist does not mean that I am angry at the Southern Baptist Convention. I learned long ago that I can be a Baptist without being a Southern Baptist. And anyway, I got over being angry at the SBC a long time ago. Rehearsing the takeover of the Southern Baptist Convention feels to me about like going to a Civil War reenactment. What happened to my old denominational home was wrong. It was based on poor theological assumptions; it was hurtful; and it has resulted in official notions and positions that I cannot, as a matter of conscience, support. But neither can I, as a matter of conscience, stay angry at the SBC.

There are fine people who are Southern Baptists just as there are fine Methodists, Lutherans, Presbyterians, Catholics, Episcopalians, Nazarenes, Quakers, Mennonites, and Pentecostals. I can no longer think of myself as a Southern Baptist, but my inability to declare with unbridled enthusiasm my reason for being a Baptist has nothing to do with that sad old story.

My wondering is tied instead to a much larger, deeper question about denominationalism itself. There has long fermented inside me a little discomfort with multilayered denominational organizations. (They seem not to be congruent with a barefoot Galilean carpenter who had no place to lay his head.) That long ferment of discomfort has escalated and intensified in recent years as I have been seized by something I have come to call "the theology of extremity." This "theology of extremity," as it relates to denominationalism, goes something like this: As long as anyone in the world is living in extreme poverty, extreme pain, or extreme danger, how can believers justify investing enormous sums of money, energy, and time in the denominational industry? I know people in a mountain village in Honduras who are raising their children on dirt floors and have no access to dental or health care or adequate clothing, shoes, or nutrition.

Unless Jesus was just passing the time of day when he said what he said in Matthew 25, how can we justify the money we spend "in the name of Jesus" on the industry of denominational conventions and buildings in the light of the world's severe extremity? How can we justify all the time and energy denominations have spent in our narcissistic intramural debates about the fine nuances of doctrine, while people are grieving for their slain children on America's violent streets?

This theology of extremity makes me wonder hard about my own personal materialism, about the blissfully triumphalist state of the church wherever it has grown prosperous and majoritarian, and it gives me pause about the industry of denominationalism.

But I say these words softly, because there is an answer that defends denominationalism, even in the face of the theology of extremity. At their best, denominations become channels through which resources are marshaled and distributed to address the world's extremity. Denominations send missionaries, build hospitals, distribute food, build water purification systems, and construct schools—all in the name and spirit of our Lord Jesus. Denominational structures provide channels through which practical help can flow to meet extreme need. And that pragmatic role, the role of marshaling resources and responding to needs, is what justifies the existence of denominations. For me, that is the highest spiritual justification for denominationalism, Baptist or otherwise.

Denominationalism based on a sense of doctrinal superiority was once a part of my reason for being a Baptist. I honestly believed we were "right"—more right than others, most right of all. I actually assigned a sort of theological, spiritual superiority to being Baptist. That was the basis of my denominationalism. But no longer.

I still believe what Baptists believe. I passionately embrace the truth of every believer's access to and responsibility before God, the truth of the church "neither hindered or helped by the state," the truth of the authority of scripture interpreted in the light of the life of Christ, the truth of the autonomy of every congregation to hammer out its own path. I embrace as ardently as ever those historic Baptist ideals. But I also know that many people who aren't Baptists embrace similar notions. And I also know that, as Kirby Godsey, one of Baptists' most honest and courageous theologians, once said, "God's truth is too big for any one mind, any one church, any one denomination . . . When we get to heaven, we're going to find out we were all a little bit wrong."

Because I am sure that those words are true, I can no longer honestly profess to embrace denominationalism on the basis of "being Baptist equals being right." In fact, I often wonder if our Quaker friends aren't a little closer to "right" than we are, if "right" means following Jesus. I don't know. But I do know this: Any passion I have left for denominationalism resides in my awareness that denominations can gather and distribute resources that undergird missionaries and missions that respond to extreme need with gospel words and deeds in Jesus' name. That, it seems to me, is the only real justification for denominationalism.

My denominational tentativeness may constitute an isolated case. If so, then my testimony is purely personal and is irrelevant to the shape of the Baptist identity in the twenty-first century. If, on the other hand, my denominational doubts bear some resemblance to a larger trend, then they constitute one voice among many voices; voices that in the next century may be saying a lot about theology and the gospel but little about denominationalism of any kind, Baptist or otherwise. I don't care much for those popular "trend studies" that categorize people into generational compartments, but perhaps it is true that the World War II generation is indeed a generation of "builders" and "joiners," people who find meaning in building institutions and in "joining"—joining civic clubs, fraternal organizations, and other bodies with memberships.

If this assumption is true, it may also be true that those same "builders and joiners" were naturally concerned that their churches join and be "good members" of larger bodies. (Might that have been a bit of the sociological fuel behind the uniformity and growth of the SBC in the middle of this century?) The next two generations of adults seem less interested in "joining" and have less passion about being members of something. (Might that be a bit of the sociological chill behind the "postdenominational" generation? Perhaps when individuals don't feel much personal need to be "joiners," they don't feel as much need for their church to find its identity in membership in a larger body.)

All of this, of course, could spell peril if it leads to "lone-ranger churches," because there is much good that churches can do in cooperation that they cannot do in isolation. Can a pragmatic denominationalism emerge that results in Baptist churches combining their resources for the common good and the gospel cause, but with a mature realism that suffers from no illusion of ideological superiority? In other words, can we have the pragmatic effectiveness of denominations without the distraction of denominationalism? Perhaps that will be the shape of our Baptist identity in the twenty-first century: a denomination without denominationalism; the pragmatic good of seminaries, missionaries, and hospitals that only gathered church resources can accomplish, without the corporate egotism and embellished organizationalism of busy denominationalism. Who can say?

My denominationalism, tentative as it is, remains inside the Baptist flock. My assignment is to say why. Obviously, it isn't because I think we are closer to God than all the others. I could say it is because we have the best system of missionary response to human extremity, but while that may be so, I can't prove it. I could say I am a Baptist because I've always been one, but I'm not sure that's the deepest reason. I think, at bottom, there is something else that keeps me Baptist.

I guess when I scrape all the varnish off the question of why I a Baptist, when I get past all the answers I know I'm expected to give, when I descend to the depths of unadorned honesty, the simple truth is that I am a Baptist today because that is where my debts are. When the lights are off, and the house is asleep, and the world is still, that is the honest truth. I am a Baptist because that is where I have an outstanding balance.

I am deep in debt to Baptist people, living and dead, who shaped my life, colored my eyes, opened my mind, and stretched my soul: John Smyth, Thomas Helwys, William Carey, E. Y. Mullins, and a long line of saints who across the centuries gave themselves to gospel principles that we now call "Baptist principles." I am in debt to Dan Barfield and Leona Evans for showing me where the Lottie Moon missionaries were on the plastic globe on top of the upright piano in the fellowship hall at Log Cabin Baptist Church in Macon, Georgia. I am in debt to Ches Smith and Howard Giddens for not writing me off when I was an "angry fundamentalist" college student. I am in debt to Cecil Sherman and John Carlton and Jim Bruner for showing me a whole new way to think about scripture, God, and church. I am in debt to Mercer University and the old Southeastern Baptist Theological Seminary, Baptist institutions that pushed, prodded, and changed my life. I am in debt to a host of sisters and brothers in Macon, Georgia, and Washington, D.C., and North Carolina and Jackson, Mississippi—women and men who have embodied our Lord's spirit in wonderful ways, women and men who happened to be Baptists, but who would have been just as committed to Christ had they been nurtured in some other stripe of the faith.

I owe much to others who belong to other traditions. That "beyond Baptist" list is a long one. But my Baptist debts start the earliest and run the deepest. Thus, I have remained. Not because I think Baptists have gotten it all right. Not because I think it's going to matter one bit when the last day comes, or that my being Baptist gets me on God's good side. And not because I think Baptists need me. Far from it. The reason I am yet a Baptist is that I have deep, long, tender debts that I owe to a long list of Baptist people, Baptist churches, and Baptist schools, and those are the kind of debts that it takes one a lifetime to repay.

So I am still here, mainly because it seems like the right thing to do, what with my being so deep in debt and all. I have serious doubts about what Jesus would think of denominationalism. I have my doubts about the way we Baptists worship at the altar of growth, programs, and activities. I have my doubts about our Baptist busyness, which too often leaves us lacking in spirituality and reflection. I have all those doubts. But I also have these debts. And my debts run deeper than my doubts. My debts weigh more than my doubts. My doubts will probably always keep me somewhere near the exit door, but my debts will probably always keep me somewhere inside the Baptist room.* Amen.

*In another context, in a taped sermon, Fred Craddock speaks of those who "sit near the exit door." His phrase spawned my thought.

Defying Definition

John Thomas Porter

It is a real challenge to state verbally why I am a Baptist. It is more difficult to articulate through the written word reasons why one is a Baptist, and not sound confused, irrational, illogical, and insensitive.

I would like to be considered a sound theologian, a scholarly teacher, a sensitive pastor, and an intellectual. But the truth is, I am none of these.

I was born a Missionary Baptist, or would it be more correct to say, "I was baptized into the Baptist church at an early age. (Missionary Baptists are predominantly black churches.)

During the latter years of my ministerial journey I led my congregation to form a dual alliance with National Baptists and Southern Baptists, which was not possible in previous years. The dual alliance raised many questions in the minds of both blacks and whites. Even a good friend from seminary who had never written me a letter of congratulations or commendation wrote me a scathing three-page letter criticizing our decision to affiliate with the Southern Baptist Convention.

Such a decision on the part of any Baptist congregation is at the core of what drives my pride in being a Baptist. The autonomy of the local congregation is the one aspect of Baptist life that I hold close and dear. This I believe is the essence of that which we are about. Each congregation has the responsibility to know and to reflect the spirit of Christ. Therefore every decision made, every mission undertaken, and every ministry promoted should be under the anointing of the Holy Spirit. The richness of being Baptist is that the autonomy of each church family is respected and appreciated. The miracle is that, beyond the individuality, common ground is found upon which the many can participate and address the larger issues.

The freedom I enjoy as a Baptist is the kind I would love to pass on to others. It is not always possible, for there are those who would take refuge in differences and are threatened by those who are not like themselves. I thank God that I have lived to see denominations move closer and closer together, leaving behind those things that once separated us and joining together in Christlike love to lift fallen humanity. I have discovered that we can worship on Saturday or Sunday in many different ways and then come together on Monday and do the will of God as it has been revealed.

Being a part of the minority community, and knowing the importance of the presence of freedom or the absence of it, gives me a high appreciation for the autonomy of the local congregation.

Over the years I have seen Baptist congregations move decisively and quickly to address a pressing social need without consulting with or seeking permission from some other authority. Guided by a determination to do the right thing, the church family has united as the people of God and made a difference in the life of the community.

In the1960s the movement to affirm the rights of all people in the United States was led by Baptists. Members of the Baptist clergy and laity were at the forefront of that movement to make the teachings of our Lord real in the lives of people. The pain suffered in southern Baptist pulpits has never been written about. I am very proud of those soldiers of Christ who stood and were counted.

I have seen the advantage of a local congregation's calling its pastor and retaining his services as long as the relationship is good and productive. I have been the pastor of this congregation for thirty-six good years.

As a Baptist, I am especially proud of the fact that we boast not about what we have, but about who we have. In the words of John Oxenham:

> Not what, but whom, I do believe,
> That in my darkest hour of need
> Hath comfort that no mortal creed
> To mortal man can give.

Not what, but whom
For Christ is more than all the creeds,
His full life of noble deeds,
Shall all the creeds outlive.

Not what I do believe, but whom;
Who walks beside me in the gloom,
Who shares the burden wearisome,
Who all the dim way doth illume,
And bids me look beyond the tomb,

The larger life to live.

Not what I do believe, but whom;
Not what, but whom.

As a Baptist, I have great faith in people and in the capacity of the local congregation to read and interpret the Scriptures and determine the way that it should live out its commitment to the work of Christ in the world.

The God-given right to make that determination should not be surrendered or negated. The opportunity for a local congregation to think and reason together and ultimately to decide is what I love most about being a Baptist.

Last but not least, I am especially proud of the wide range afforded us in the choice of liturgy. The order of services ranges from highly structured to completely spontaneous. Some Baptist congregations are very vocal in their responses to the singing and the sermon, while others are completely quiet and nonverbal in their responses. The style used to deliver the sermon varies from one church to another. This latitude in the worship service is truly Baptist and reflects the all-inclusive spirit of our Lord.

This Is My Story, This Is My Song

———— Nancy Hastings Sehested ————

Now, I know that Jesus was not a Baptist, but I have to remind myself. In my Texas Baptist Sunday school class several of us third graders had a revelation. Since John the Baptist baptized Jesus, then Jesus was a Baptist, too. Jesus was surely one of us! Such an assertion fit well within a religious ghetto that encouraged the claim that we Baptists were the best of all the rest. What further proof did we need than for Jesus to be one of us?

Years later my enlightened seminary education confirmed my earlier Sunday school insight. Jesus' baptism was a sign that he was "one of us" alright. He was one of us Gentiles and one of us Jews. One with all of us, his baptism declared the tearing down of the walls of religious nationalism and elitism. So why am I still a Baptist? After baptism, why are any of us Baptists?

I was born into the tribe of Baptists with my father and grandfather among the chief priests and scribes. My siblings and I were all schooled in the tribal ways from the Texas branch of the house of Southern Baptists. We lived by the eight-point record system that defined our lives with daily Bible readings, prayers, weekly church attendance, and offerings. We pledged allegiance to the Bible alongside the pledge to the United States. Bible sword drills gave us lightening-flash ability to locate any verse in the Scriptures.

I was a member of GAs (Girl's Auxiliary), the mission education program for young girls. We were an auxiliary to the WMU (the Women's Missionary Union), where we were encouraged in our faith by strong, competent, and creative women. The women of the WMU compellingly guided us toward becoming queens of the royal court of

Jesus Christ. Queens were rulers with power and beauty. We passed through training steps that led us to the royal coronation. We learned Bible stories, cooked food from foreign lands, heard stories from missionaries in faraway places, and prayed for people whose names we could not pronounce. We memorized Bible verses together with our GA watchword. We had to know the names of our Baptist agencies and the directors of each one. We were trained to be obedient followers of Jesus and the Southern Baptist faith.

A significant rite of passage happened for me at the age of twelve. Having advanced through the steps of Maiden, Lady-in-Waiting, and Princess, I was finally crowned Queen. A coronation complete with a long white gown was the reward. I went on to achieve the highest rank, Queen-Regent-in-Service. For this title I memorized the Sermon on the Mount, cross-stitched a map of the world, and helped with Vacation Bible School in a poor neighborhood. The reward for my efforts was a jeweled cardboard crown covered in white satin and rhinestones. My scepter was a gold spray-painted wooden rod and rubber ball. My cape was green and gold satin. I was thrilled. I was treated like a queen, like Esther in the Bible. I thought that the church would always treat me like a queen if I followed my "steps" well enough.

I had learned early that even a child could hear God's voice. As a boy, Samuel heard God. I was certain that God spoke to me, too. "Speak, Lord, for thy servant heareth." Baptism at age nine was confirmation that God was calling me. Didn't God call everyone to service? Reading and rereading the biography of our Baptist missionary to China, Lottie Moon, was further encouragement to my path. She seemed fearless in her journey with God, and I loved her deeply. Her biography was titled *Her Own Way*, and I intended to follow my own way to God, too. One step led to another. At age seventeen I walked the aisle of my Baptist church and dedicated my life to "full-time" Christian service. I was a good and obedient daughter of the one true Baptist faith, ready to go into service, even if it meant going as far away as China.

Instead of China, I went much further away from home. I went into that foreign land known as ordained pastoral ministry. I was surprised that this step caused such a stir. After all, the people in the Bible had done a lot wilder things in the name of God. Twenty years ago, as a seminary graduate, I could not find work in a Baptist church. It has not been an easy path. In 1987 my entrance into Memphis, Tennessee, as pastor of Prescott Memorial Baptist Church caused the local Southern Baptist association to disfellowship the church. The motion to dismiss us stated that the church "had violated the word of God by calling a woman as pastor." The event illustrated how passionate Baptists can be over different interpretations of the same Scripture. Yet it is the same passion that has led some Baptists to follow their faith where others fear to tread.

Since I frequently traffic in ecumenical circles, I am often asked why I stay a Baptist. Our legendary Baptist brawls and bellyaches are enough in the news to be thought of as chronic behavior. We can count on at least one humiliating statement annually to emerge from the Southern Baptist Convention. With Jesse Helms, Jerry Falwell, and Bill Clinton all claiming the family name, the disclaimers pop out of us automatically, "But I'm not that kind of Baptist."

What kind of Baptist am I? With each passing year the question gets harder and harder to answer. But I believe it is true that I am a Baptist by temperament and sometimes even by conviction. I am feisty, passionate, and sometimes iconoclastic. I do not bend and bow to authority easily, having learned well that I have only one authority. Over the years Baptists have been both storm and refuge in my pilgrimage. Baptists have loved me and hated me with equal ferocity. I have reciprocated with a matching fervor of love and hate, pride and embarrassment.

But you see, it is from Baptists that I learned not to allow anyone but God to name and define me. From Baptists I learned that I have not only the right, but also the responsibility to read the biblical story and claim it as my story. I learned that I did not have to rely on the dictates of priest, pastor, or pope. From Baptists I learned that our ancestors sacrificed their lives to hold the freedom of individual soul competency. However incompetent my soul may be in living this story, I am free to work out my salvation with fear and trembling. I am emboldened by my Baptist ancestors who were impassioned, impatient, and impertinent before meddling state or religious authorities.

With the changes in Southern Baptist life in the past two decades, I have from time to time entertained the thought of leaving my Baptist family. But if I leave someday, I dare not leave the liberating story of God that Baptists taught me. Perhaps when history beams its light on this passage in Baptist life, we will be identified less by the battles we won or lost and more by the stories we loved and lived.

The story I love is the story of God's love dwelling smack dab in the middle of the mess of our lives. This radical, life-altering story of Christ still compels me. I like singing the "blood" hymns in our earthier churches. Other religious groups may have their order and mystery, but we have blood. It is scandalous. It is messy. It gets outrageous at times. We sing "Nothing but the Blood of Jesus" as part of a long tradition that knows the bloody truth. It costs to follow Jesus. Some of our own blood may spill.

We know the story. We sing the song. The bloody scene of death when truth and falsehood collide, when freedom and oppression battle, is not the final word. We know that all flesh is grass, even that growing up like weeds around our Baptist principles. But we also know that death is the prelude to new life. For us, this story is given ritual form in our ordinance of baptism. I know that it is not the amount of water that is the saving grace. However, it is the excess of water that has kept me a Baptist. I am baptized. I am drenched in God. I am a follower of the Christ who "does not fail or get discouraged until justice has been established in the earth" (Isa 42:4) This is my story. This is my song.

Hard Times Make for Hard Thinking

—— *Cecil E. Sherman* ——

L ike most of the people who contributed to this book, I was born
Baptist, and especially Southern Baptist. On both sides of my family
Baptist roots are long and deep. So, when I told my wife, Dot, I was
writing a piece about why I am a Baptist, she said, "Why don't you tell
the truth? Your parents were Baptist. That's why you are a Baptist." And
as usual, Dot is right. The article could stop right here.

If it did, I would not pass to the future any record of a painful journey that was forced upon many of us who have had to rethink the
Baptist idea. In the last twenty years thousands of loyal Southern
Baptists have been officially marginalized—actually, we've been
trashed. We have no voice in making policy for missions, theological
education, or ministries. Most galling, we can't use the machinery of a
denomination to argue our position. We are nonpersons. Our predica-
ment is a consequence of being "losers" in a long and ugly war for
control of the Southern Baptist denomination.

"The war" was about more than power; it was about powerful ideas
that are at the heart of "being Baptist." The ideas of the winners are
now on the table. They are taught at Southern Baptist seminaries,
thundered from pulpits that "speak for Southern Baptists," and printed
by Broadman Press. The losers have had to create seminaries to teach
their ideas and establish new publishing ventures to get their ideas
before the public.

Our situation is unique to our history. We write to "explain" ourselves. We write to argue a "Baptist point of view." Other generations
have done as much. But again, our situation is unique. Here's how.

In England and America in the seventeenth and eighteenth centuries, Baptists wrote to hostile governments and an uninformed public to explain what it meant to be Baptists. They argued for freedom of conscience and separation of church and state. In the nineteenth century, especially in America, denominations competed with one another. Baptists entered debates to argue against infant baptism and for baptism by immersion. The competition was Methodists, Presbyterians, and the Church of Christ. This spirit lingers only in backwaters today. But it was in this environment that Baptists 150 years ago explained themselves and Baptist ideas.

Today "our kind" of Baptists are in a strange world. The people who have handled us roughly call themselves Baptists, and they now possess the property and titles of a vast Baptist denomination. To a half-informed public, they are Baptists. And if they are Baptists, then who are they? To further complicate matters, we live in a time when denominational labels are becoming near worthless. A younger generation doesn't care about Baptist, Methodist, or any other denomination. To write about "being Baptist" as if it were important is off the mark. In this sort of climate we tell our story and redefine what it means to be Baptist.

At my parents' table I learned Baptist ideas. From Stewart Newman at Southwestern Baptist Theological Seminary I learned about being Baptist. At Princeton Theological Seminary I had to "explain" Baptists to Presbyterians. But all that was a primer for what would follow. Baptist theory is one thing; Baptist ideas in real life are another. It is like the difference between studying about football and playing the game or studying about war and fighting a war. I had studied Baptist ideas, but I rethought those ideas in "the war." Those ideas included the following.

Experienced Religion

I sat across the table from a "big" preacher. His church had five thousand on a Sunday morning. I asked him about his evangelism strategy. He said his church employed two seminary students, each of whom was required to have two people come forward for baptism each Sunday. Therefore, a minimum of four people would "profess faith" each Sunday—208 a year. He added, "You can't get invitations to evangelism conferences unless you baptize 200 a year." I was dumbfounded!

I probed a bit. "What if Sunday comes and the seminarian doesn't have two who will profess faith?" He responded, "I will get students who can get the job done." I questioned, "What if these fellows are forced to cut some theological corners to meet their quota?" He was unconcerned and thought my question trivial, pesky, and the child of too lively a conscience.

Forced evangelism—"count-em" evangelism—steals Baptist stuff. At one time everyone was baptized only days after their birth. Everyone was a member of the church. The Baptist idea was to claim again a reborn church membership, to insure that all in the congregation were actually "saved." We asked each person to bear witness to an experience with Jesus, and then we baptized them. Much of modern evangelism counts "converts" and advances the careers of ambitious preachers. Experienced religion is God-driven, not pressured. The Spirit of God is not programmed. These ideas were at work in the church of my childhood, but times changed, and I had to rethink experienced religion.

Authoritarian Preachers and Ordinary People

Growing up in the United States, authoritarian was a foreign word, a part of another time and place. In Europe three hundred years ago people struggled with the divine right of kings, but that was long ago, I thought. But I was wrong.

There came a time when I was put on the Southern Baptist Peace Committee. The group was misnamed, however. We didn't make peace; we advanced the cause of one side in "the war." In that group I saw the authoritarian preacher at work. He knows the mind of God. He knows what the Bible means. He speaks for God. He does not err, and he knows error when others speak it.

I grew up in a climate where the preacher had considerable influence. But the preacher was one voice; the laity also could know the mind of God and the sense of the Scriptures. Dignity, competency, fairness, and tolerance were built into our congregational system. The possibility that I might be wrong was always kept in mind. My father taught me to ponder what the preacher said. He was usually to be honored, but the preacher could be wrong. I was taught to use my head and think for myself.

Then I met preachers who claimed to know the mind of God and so made themselves rulers of the church. Maybe authoritarianism was not so remote after all. If preachers speak for God, then the idea of congregationalism is nonexistent. A people called Baptists fled authoritarianism a long time ago. Now I know why.

Congregationalism

Around the edges of all I've been writing is the way Baptists sort things out. If ordinary people can read and interpret the Bible (and that is the premise lay Sunday School teachers stand on), and if decisions are made at the annual church meeting by the vote of all members of a Baptist church, then we have vested ordinary people with real power. It is true that most members don't exercise the power; they avoid church business meetings like a contagious disease. But happily, some members do take to heart their chance to have a say in the way a church does its work.

Suppose a congregation decides to ordain a woman to the ministry? Where is the Baptist rule book? How can we know whether this congregation is out of bounds or not? Luckily, built into Baptist life is congregationalism. That means a local congregation gets to read the New Testament and decide what it means. Together the pastor and laity think, pray, and make a decision. Working from such premise would result in diversity among Baptist congregations. And there was.

But in 1979 there came a group who were troubled by diversity; they insisted upon much more uniformity. Congregations that were "out of line" would be disciplined. Churches were put out of associations. Other churches were no longer fit to send representatives to sit on boards of seminaries or mission-sending agencies. They were excluded, for they did not conform to rules made by national bodies. "Correct theology" was determined at the national convention. If you want to know how you should think about the Bible, don't read church history or study the work of scholars. Rather, get a copy of a resolution passed at a national convention in 1981. That's the way you are to think.

What happened to congregationalism? It does not matter. Baptist precedent does not inform or concern these people. We must say the right words and require everyone who is in good standing to say them with us. In that climate I had to rethink where Baptist decisions are made. If national bodies are more likely to get it right than local congregations, then maybe we need popes and councils to protect us from ourselves. But if ordinary people can interpret the Bible and think through how to do church, then the Baptist idea needs to live.

✝✝✝✝

I believe people have dignity and innate good sense. God didn't send Jesus to save us and trust the church into our care because we were incompetents. God in Christ trusted the church into the care of devout fishermen. All of us are successors to those fishermen—men and women, old and young, college professors and barbers, grocery checkers and CPAs. Since God believed in us, why can't we believe in each other and give each other a little space?

I've seen people abused. When the SBC in session voted women second-class status, I saw my sister-in-law beat on the chest of the chair of the Resolutions Committee that brought the stupid resolution. With tears streaming down her face, she filed a protest. She was a person. She was made in the image of God. She didn't have to ride in the back of the Baptist bus. What had happened hurt. She was telling us her pain.

I know a little of how she felt. I pled for fairness from the Peace Committee, but I was in the minority. My voice counted for nothing. I had never been ignored or made powerless. Institutions I had loved and cared for all my life were being taken over and put beyond my reach. It hurt. And in that pain I had to think again what it means to be Baptist.

One illustration says it all. At the Southern Baptist Convention meeting in New Orleans in June 1990, I sat in the balcony and watched and listened. In a business session a man said something that offended the presiding officer. The officer flipped a switch, the mike went dead, and the voice was gone. The offending voice was silenced, didn't count, could not argue his position before the house. It was power like that used by a medieval king or bishop. A simple majority had made a tyrant of the president. A minority could not state his position.

Fast-forward to August 1990. About three thousand Southern Baptists met in Atlanta. We were a fragment of the minority that had gathered in New Orleans two months earlier. We could not speak in New Orleans, so we had our own meeting to vent our feelings. Daniel Vestal presided over the Atlanta meeting. A man came to a floor mike. He made a poor case for a poor idea. When he finished, he had made no motion. He began to shuffle back to his seat. The house could go on to better ideas (and more important people). But Daniel Vestal was not content with the way the scenario was playing out. He called the man back and said, "Sir, you made no motion, and I must go to the next item of business unless we can get your idea on the floor. Can I help you make a motion of your idea?" The man came back to the mike. He and Daniel (before us all) made a motion of his idea. Daniel then turned to Charles Wade and said, "Charles, second that motion." Charles was on the platform. Wade protested saying, "I'm not for the motion." Daniel said, "Second it anyway." There came a meek second to the motion. Then with dignity and patience Daniel Vestal let the man have his say in support of his motion. The motion failed. The man counted. He was a person. He had a voice, a chance. It was one of the most Baptist things I've ever seen.

"Baptist" is not so much about theology. Baptists have offered precious little theology to the world. Catholics, Lutherans, and Presbyterians have written most of our theology (and I am grateful). But being Baptist is about the way people are treated. God invested a lot in ordinary people; we ought to be willing to do as much. It's the Baptist way to do church.

We live in a confusing time. Churches that call themselves Baptist are as authoritarian as ever a Roman Church was. Pastors function as archbishops. Lay people shaken by the affronts of aggressive secularism want a "certainty merchant" in the pulpit. Those who live in a "bottom line" world bring that mentality to church. They want results, numbers, and growth. They don't worry about details such as priesthood of the believer and separation of church and state. But dotted around this strange landscape are people who have lived through the wars, gotten over the pain, and rethought the Baptist idea. We may never be so large as the old SBC, but maybe we don't need to be. Holding on to ideas about the worth of a person and the fairness of a system may be as important as dollars and numbers. I believe John Smyth and Thomas Helwys might recognize us as kin, and if that be so, maybe our pain has served us well.

Second Baptist Church, Greenville, Mississippi

——— *Walter B. Shurden* ———

Walter B. Shurden

Filled with very common people with untrained voices, the robeless choir hummed in the background while M. E. Perry leaned into the microphone, almost whispering with that Godlike bass voice:

> Welcome to the Sunday morning broadcast of the Second Baptist Church in Greenville, Mississippi. We are glad you have joined us by radio and invite you to come worship with us in person at 907 South Theobald Street. We are the church "where friends meet friends and sinners meet Christ," and where you are always welcome.

After a few more sentences of trying to entice radio land to come our way, he would close,

> Once again, we are the Second Baptist Church, 907 South Theobald, Greenville, Mississippi, M. E. Perry, pastor.

Turning from the microphone toward the choir, he slipped out of his preacher role and into his minister of music portfolio, conducting the choir as they began singing the lyrics they had been humming. It was the Second Baptist Church's call to worship. M. E. Perry wrote it, and I have hummed and sung it to myself for forty-five years:

> Because Christ Jesus died for me,
> because he suffered on a tree,
> because he lived and died for me,
> I consecrate my all.

In that simple manner I was introduced into the immeasurably rich liturgy of the Christian tradition. It was also my introduction into the Baptist tradition.

Surely the unstated assumption in a book with the title *Why I Am a Baptist* is that, after extolling Baptist ideas and ideals, we writers will eventually get around to telling you that we are Baptists because of "Baptist beliefs." The most vulgar form of that is, "Baptists are closer to the New Testament than others, so I joined and stayed on." A more palatable form goes like this: "I am a Baptist because I grew up Baptist, but in my mature years I also learned the truthfulness of Baptist ideas." None of the first and only a bit of that latter kind of thing is in my story, and I will get around to it in time. But honesty compels me to start at a very different point.

"Second"

I am a Baptist partly because of economics. My mother finished the tenth grade; my daddy quit after the fourth. At the time of his death his eighty-four-year-old crusty and gnarled hands testified that he had worked long and hard as a welder and pipefitter. He could barely read the words in the hymnbook. I was the first person in my nuclear family to graduate from college and the first in my extended family to receive a doctorate.

My family was what I braggingly described as "lower middle class." Truth be told, we were probably one-rung below that! The only time I can remember really being embarrassed by our standing in life was in my early years of high school. Our family had one car—an old blue Chevrolet with one black fender! My brother and I would ask our mother and daddy to let us out a block or two from high school. We needed exercise, we said. As now, status mattered then to adolescents.

Move me a tad down the socioeconomic ladder in the Delta of Mississippi in the 1950s, and I would probably have ended up with the Church of God or Pentecostals, which would have been fine, I am sure. For certain I would not have been an Episcopalian or Presbyterian, not even a Methodist. As it was, I first experienced the Holy in life in my dormitory room in the spring of my first year of college. I committed my life to Christ and promptly asked for membership in the Second Baptist Church of Greenville, Mississippi, my parents' home church.

Don't let the "Second" part of that church name slip by you. We were "second" not merely in terms of chronology; we were "second" in terms of zip codes, the vehicles we drove, the English we spoke, and the jobs we worked at. We worked for the folks at "First" Baptist Church. Baptists are stratified sociologically just as denominations are.[1] The people at "First Church"—people I later admired—had a beautiful carpeted sanctuary with plush cushions in the pews and beautiful robes on the choir members. But at Second Church we knew liberalism when we saw it! We had concrete floors, hard wooden pews to punish the body for the sins of the soul, and nobody in our choir wore a robe. Formalism, we said at Second Baptist, was the death of the spirit. Being antiformal was one way we had of being superior!

Our preacher, "Brother" M. E. Perry, pranced up and down the rostrum, occasionally strayed into the church aisles, clapped his hands, and preached six octaves louder than "Dr." Perry Claxton at First Baptist Church. Both Perrys, thankfully, became fathers-in-God to me. As with most ecclesiastical stratification, economics, not theology, served as the primary wedge between First and Second Baptist Churches in Greenville, Mississippi. At Second Baptist Church we *accepted* our "second" status. We accepted it socially, economically, and educationally. But we took second place to no group religiously.

In his well-used history of Baptists, Robert G. Torbet attributed Baptist growth in America to its appeal to "plain people." Please do not mistake this description for an inverted social elitism; it is not. But to be sure, some Baptists have wallowed in their "plainness." You know, "Aw shucks, I am just an old country boy," when what they really mean is, "I am just a *good* ole country boy!" But to say as Torbet did that Baptist growth was due to its appeal to "plain people" is not sociological brag; it is historical truth, especially in the southern part of the United States.

I once asked Emmanuel McCall, an African-American Baptist, what he and I, so different in our background and culture, had in common as Baptists. He answered, "We are common folks." Let's be sure of what we are talking about and describing here. We are talking "once upon a time."

Baptists have pulled a massive comeuppance in the world of American religion.[2] We now have some Episcopalian money, and a few Baptists have Book-of-Common-Prayer liturgies. We even have some

Presbyterian education! (We had much more superb education until the fundamentalists among us tried choking the life out of the University of Richmond, Wake Forest, Furman, Stetson, Baylor, Carson-Newman, and a few others. Consequently, these stellar schools exited the Baptist scene.) And we have Catholic influence. Look at the faces that dominate Washington, D.C.: Bill Clinton, Al Gore, Trent Lott, Newt Gingrich, Strom Thurmond, Robert Byrd, Jesse Helms, and Jesse Jackson. They are all Baptists! Blaming the Jews in New York or the liberals in the Ivy-League East for the mess in the country simply no longer works!

But the issue is more than denominational; it is personal. I now prefer stately anthems to some of the down-home gospel singing I cut my teeth on at Second Baptist, though the latter can still stir my heart. I prefer silence and a richer liturgy to the boisterous fellowship and simple worship of earlier years. And I prefer to hear the pulpit struggle with the ambiguities and contradictions of life rather than to proclaim, however so enthusiastically, the simplicities I first confused with the gospel. For me, this is not comeuppance; it is spiritual growth and discovery, the discovery of *mystery*.

My saga in Baptist churches is, again thankfully, as diverse as Baptist life itself. I've worshiped "high," "low," "broad," and what my friend Bill Leonard calls "charismatic lite" (hands but no tongues!). I've sung out of both the front and back of the *Baptist Hymnal* and from every kind of hymnbook, including Stamps-Baxter. I've preached in coatless short sleeve dress shirts in rural frame buildings and in Geneva gowns in urban cathedrals; spotted lots of "first" folks in "second" churches and lots of "second" folks in "first" churches; baptized in cow ponds, cold rivers, and warm "indoor" baptismal pools; and been part of Sunday morning worship that closed with as much as forty-three verses of "Just As I Am" and as little as a brief benediction.

I came out of Second Baptist Church in Greenville, Mississippi, but I spent several years at St. Charles Avenue Baptist Church in New Orleans, Louisiana, Crescent Hill Baptist Church in Louisville, Kentucky, and even a couple of months at the cathedral at Myers Park Baptist Church in Charlotte, North Carolina. To say it historically for those who know the references, I came out of Sandy Creek, but I've been to Charleston. I apologize for neither and am grateful that Baptists have been "catholic" enough to have both and all shades in between. Indeed, I am glad that at the beginning of a new millennium we Baptists have churches of all kinds. Rich kids need to know that Jesus loves them just as do "lower middle class" kids. But being lower middle class, I started at "Second" Baptist. Economics is partly responsible for my Baptist beginnings.

"Church"

I am Baptist partly because of emotions. We were "Second" Baptist Church on South Theobald in Greenville, Mississippi, but we were also Second Baptist "Church." Sociologists delight in telling you that the "Second" part of our name probably made church out of us more than the "Church" part of our name. To say it another way, people choose the churches they do because of acceptance and a sense of belonging.

H. Richard Niebuhr made that point way back in 1929 in *The Social Sources of Denominationalism*. Now read Niebuhr's title again. There is truth in it! Christian denominations have social, not just theological, differences. At Second Baptist we were "Church" because we accepted each other, cared for each other, and belonged to each other. And doubtless our ease of belonging, what we called our "fellowship," surely had something, as Niebuhr said, to do with our "second" status. We were with our kind. We may have been "Second" to those on the outside, but we were "Church" to each other on the inside.

After he announced his intention not to seek the presidency a second term and so to return to his ranch in Texas, Lyndon Johnson was asked by someone why he was leaving the power and pomp of Washington to return to Texas. He said, "Because out there they ask about you when you are sick, and they cry when you die." That's what those plain people did at Second "Church."

Even though I did not grow up at the church's altar, the plain people at Second Baptist Church in Greenville, Mississippi, became "church" to me when I was age eighteen. That is the second reason I am a Baptist. Economics may have been an unconscious force in my becoming a Baptist, but I was totally conscious of being loved. I am a Baptist partly because of emotions. Baptist people were the first

Christians to love me. Had I gone to a Church of God or a Methodist church and had they loved me as did those wonderful people down on South Theobald, I doubtless would have ended up one of them rather than one of us.

Along with those carpetless concrete floors at Second Baptist Church, we had rip-roaring gospel singing (much of which I can still do pretty well at from memory), revved-up evangelistic preaching, hugs and tears, and a place that *felt* unspeakably, indescribably good to me. The only appropriate word to describe the place is one we would have never used at Second Baptist, even if we had known it— "sanctuary!" A sanctuary is a holy or sacred place, a refuge, an asylum, a shelter. More than anything else, this particular "sanctuary" on South Theobald consisted of a somewhat uneducated, more than somewhat unwealthy, lily-white, uncritical people who claimed to hate sin and Satan but love God, Jesus, the Bible, each other, and me.

What made Second Baptist Church feel unspeakably and indescribably good, of course, was overwhelmingly personal. Either those people loved me, believed in me, wanted the best for me, or they have deceived me to this very moment. I will always believe the former. Looking back over my shoulder after more than forty-five years, I realize how much at eighteen I resembled all eighteen-year-olds, thinking secretly that I was nobody and wanting so very much to be somebody.

Reverberating within the walls of that simple but blessed sanctuary of Second Baptist Church on South Theobald in Greenville, Mississippi, I heard the affirming whispers of those plain people, "You are somebody. You really are somebody!" Fortunately, it is difficult, even impossible, to get over being loved. And those people launched me with love! They launched me not only into life but also into the ministry of Jesus Christ. For the three years I was at Mississippi College (a Baptist college) in undergraduate school, that struggling little Baptist church sent a check every month for thirty-five dollars (good money in those days) to the college's finance office to help pay my tuition. Moreover, they did it for the other seven preacher-boys who came out of that church during the same period of time. Incidentally, a church that is not appealing enough to produce women and men for the ministry needs to check its spiritual pulse.

"Baptist"

I am a Baptist first because of economics and second because of emotions. But third, I am a Baptist because I was educated to be one. I am a Baptist because I learned to be.

The first Baptist book I ever read was Joe T. Odle's *A Church Member's Handbook*, replete with historical, theological, and denominational silliness, for example, "successionism." Successionism is the perverse idea that Baptists are the true church because they can trace themselves back to the Jordan River and John the Baptist. That's where I began Christian nurture, being taught the theological tribalism that Baptists are the true church.

I was a heretic from the beginning; I never believed it. However, while I may never have believed we were the only ones, I snuggled up pretty close to the absurdity that we were the best ones, but I have repented of that a thousand times and with good reason. Tribalism, like all other provincialisms, has to die. I do not decry the death of tribalism, but neither do I deny the pull of home. For me, the larger Baptist family has been my home and my little corner of the forty-acre field of Christendom. I hope I am not flirting again with tribalism when I say that at the center of my being there is something about being Baptist as I understand it that is both freeing and fulfilling. What is that?

It is the principle of voluntarism. My wife tells me not to use that word because it does not communicate. But the abortion debate has conscripted the word "choice." And when I tried using the word "freedom" for a synonym, a few Baptists thought that I was shucking responsibility while others accused me of being, as they said, "too anthropocentric rather than theocentric." Both had misunderstood, of course. But let's try voluntarism this time.

• Voluntarism—Authentic faith is chosen as God works through the individual's will.

• Voluntarism—Coercion of any kind and all kinds is out.

• Voluntarism—If faith is to be valid, it must be uncoerced.

• Voluntarism—The only conversion that counts is conversion by conviction.

- Voluntarism—Where there is no autonomy, there is no authenticity.

- Voluntarism—Cramming a creed down a person's throat is rape of the soul.

We Baptists do not distinguish ourselves from other Christian groups by our concepts of God, Christ, the Holy Spirit, and other such cardinal Christian emphases. We don't have a Baptist bible, separate from other Christians. Nor do we identify ourselves by certain theological approaches, for example, Calvinism with its stress on the sovereignty of God or Arminianism with its emphasis on human free will. Both Calvinism and Arminianism have long and noble histories among Baptists, but one can be either or neither and still be a Baptist. Nor are we distinguished by popular theological labels. Among Baptists you will find fundamentalists, conservatives, liberals, evangelicals, and everything in between. But it is a serious mistake and gross misrepresentation of our history to equate "Baptist" with any of these. One can be a Baptist and be any of these.

I am a Baptist because the core value of the Baptist vision of Christianity is voluntarism. Freedom. Choice. Here is what voluntarism means for me in relation to the individual, the church, the state, and religious authority.

In terms of Christian discipleship, this means I personally, individually, and voluntarily choose to follow Christ. No one imposes this on me—not God, the church, my family, or the state. Saved completely by God's grace and not by my doings, I accept God's grace, submit to God's will, and with other believers start my Christian journey. Negatively, this means I do not believe that one becomes a Christian automatically, sacramentally, or institutionally through baptism or the Lord's Supper. I am drawn to the Baptist insistence on believer's baptism because it stems from the belief that baptism, representing one's commitment to Christ, is freely chosen. On the other hand, Baptist opposition to infant baptism stems from the belief that infants cannot choose and that proxy faith is no faith at all. I am a Baptist because I believe that the Christian faith is personal, experiential, and voluntary.

In terms of the church, Baptist voluntarism means that I voluntarily covenant with others who have trusted Christ as Savior and Lord, and under God's Spirit we create together a believers' church. Faith begins privately, in the lonely soul of the individual, but it is rooted in a congregation of believers. I like the idea that Baptist Christians who voluntarily covenant with each other to form a local church are free, under the Lordship of Christ, to determine our membership, which we insist should be of believers only. Calling this a "regenerate church membership," we seek to safeguard that membership through believer's baptism by immersion. The "believers" part of the baptism is far more important to me than the "immersion" part. Moreover, in our churches we Baptists choose our leadership, order our worship and work, ordain whom we wish, and voluntarily participate in the larger body of Christ. Without priesthood or hierarchy, we affirm that all members of the churches stand on equal footing and serve as priests before God, to the church, and for the world.

As a local Baptist church under the Lordship of Christ and the word of Holy Scripture, we are an autonomous, self-governing body. We practice congregational church polity. We are also an independent body, fully the church without reference to some larger institution. However, we Baptists voluntarily unite with other churches in covenant relationships through associational, regional, and national denominational bodies. Moreover, we Baptists see our churches and all other Christian churches as part of the universal Church of Jesus Christ. I am a Baptist because I believe the local church is a covenanted community of believers responsible under God for its life and faith, but I also believe the universal church of Jesus Christ includes all of God's people everywhere.

In terms of the state, Baptist voluntarism makes me an ardent advocate of liberty of conscience and opinion, including freedom of religion, freedom for religion, and freedom from religion. We Baptists have championed religious liberty because of our belief that God alone is Lord of the conscience. Also, we have led the religious liberty parade because we have insisted that if faith is to be genuine, it must be free. Because this kind of voluntarism works best where religion and government are separate, Baptists have argued historically for the separation of church and state. I am a Baptist because I believe in liberty of conscience for every human being and because I oppose the entanglement of government and religion, recognizing, of course, that complete separation is impossible.

In terms of religious authority, Baptists, as do most other Christians, point to the authority of scripture for faith and practice. Unlike many other Christians, however, Baptists do not invest the final interpretation of the Bible in creeds, councils, or clergy. Certainly the interpretations of creed, councils, and clergy cannot be imposed. We Baptists leave the Bible where it belongs. It belongs in the hands of the individual believer, who interprets it within the trusting relationship of a local congregation of believers. This does not mean that Baptists can believe anything they want and remain Baptists. It does mean, however, that the Bible is a dynamic, not a static or closed, book. Its final interpretation is not locked up in ancient creeds or confessions or in the hands of a few ecclesiastical specialists. I am a Baptist because as anticreedalists, Baptists believe in an open Bible and an open mind, both working in the context of trusting relationships in a local church.

All of these distinctives and some I have not listed are vulnerable to the Confuser, Clarence Jordan's word for Satan. The authority of scripture can be tragically distorted into blind biblicism and excessive subjectivism. Baptist individualism can be transformed into the sovereignty of self and narcissistic privatism, and the independence and autonomy of the local church into ecclesiastical lone-rangerism. Liberty of conscience can easily degenerate into expediency rather than principle, prostituting itself into freedom for "us" or for "Christians" or for "Americans."

These distortions are not only possible; sadly, they have occurred in Baptist history. This important principle of freedom or voluntarism can easily get lost. It can be sacrificed on the altars of political ideologies that are only inches from governmental tyranny. It can get so enmeshed in culture, it never recognizes that it has become a ruthless system of domination. It can be conscripted as a code word for self-serving caucuses and one-eyed movements. It can lose itself, as non-Baptist Langdon Gilkey said, in the trivia of self-indulgence.[3] It can get lost in corporatism and a pack mentality. Voluntarism—freedom—the Baptist vision—is an exceedingly fragile commodity.

But I live with the conviction that voluntarism represents the Baptist heritage. I am hopeful that the core value of voluntarism will survive and triumph as the prevailing Baptist vision. Philip Jacob Spener, the spearhead of German Pietism and a resounding critic of German Lutheranism of the seventeenth century, requested a few days before his death that he be buried in a white rather than a black coffin. He had lamented sufficiently the condition of the church while on earth, he said. In dying he wanted a white coffin, symbolic of his hope for a better church on earth. I have that kind of optimism for Baptists.

At bottom I believe that "voluntarism" or "freedom" or "choice"—call it what you will—is temporarily conquerable and subject to perversion. I also believe, however, that it is an ultimately imperishable moral commodity. That is why I believe that, even if Baptists sacrifice the spirit of voluntarism on pagan altars, it will rise again in some wing of the Christian church. I am a Baptist because I learned that voluntarism is the core value of Baptists.

Greenville, Mississippi

Had I been born and reared in Boston, Massachusetts, I might be a Congregationalist or a Catholic. Had I grown up in Minneapolis, Minnesota, I would probably be a Lutheran. But I am a Southerner, born in Greenwood, Mississippi, where we lived until we moved fifty-five miles far away to Greenville, Mississippi. Other places of residence: Clinton, Mississippi; Lake Village, Arkansas; New Orleans, Louisiana; Ruston, Louisiana; Jefferson City, Tennessee; Louisville, Kentucky; and Macon, Georgia. Look at that! Mississippi, Arkansas, Louisiana, Tennessee, Kentucky, and Georgia! When the Southeastern Conference plays, I can't lose! But neither do I know for whom to root! But more to the point, it is difficult to grow up where I grew up or live all your life where I have lived without either being a Baptist, being witnessed to by a Baptist, being influenced by Baptists, or downright despising Baptists.

In a cry of despair a rather irreligious gubernatorial candidate in Mississippi, who was taking a pummeling from Baptists, once said, "Johnson grass and Baptists are taking over this state." He obviously did not know that by the time he uttered his lament, Baptists had already taken over the South. The South is my home. Environment has something to do with why I am a Baptist.

Actually my wife, three children, and I lived one exceedingly happy year in Hamilton, Ontario, Canada where Ivan Morgan, Gerry Harrop, Russell Aldwinckle, Jim Perkins, and a few others broadened my Baptistness and challenged my southernness. If they had needed a church history professor at McMaster Divinity School, we probably would have stayed and become Canadians, people we came to love and admire. But Providence or the tug of home—probably economics— shuttled us back south. A twenty-nine-year-old with a wife and three children tends to go where the work is, though those of us in the ministry downplay economics and call it the "will of God!"

I came home to the South; I was a Southern Baptist. I served as pastor of the First Baptist Church of Ruston, Louisiana (note the upward mobility from "Second Baptist" to "First Baptist"), taught seven wonderful years at a Baptist college in East Tennessee (Carson-Newman College), taught and tinkered with administration in a Baptist seminary (The Southern Baptist Theological Seminary), and taught at a Baptist university (Mercer). If all that does not make one a Southern Baptist, what does?

But in June 1987 I divorced the Southern Baptist Convention when its fundamentalist leaders stopped being Baptist. They trashed the cardinal Baptist concept of the priesthood of all believers, subjugated women, idolized the Bible, crucified freedom, baptized the right wing of the Republican Party, and in general moved the Southern Baptist Convention just to the right of every place I wanted to be. But they had already accused me and my friends of moving to the left of every place they thought we should be! Doubtless, we both overaccused and misaccused.

The divorce, as divorces often do, liberated me. It did not send me scurrying toward the broader, more catholic Baptist tradition and toward the broader more catholic Christian church. I had been there for a long time. But it liberated me from having to defend such a decent and legitimate posture to my own denomination.

Through the years people, institutions, books, human hurts and joys, good jobs, Holy Scriptures, and Holy Spirit have worked diligently to extricate me from my parochial southern environment, my restricted Baptist education, my rustic Second Baptist Church liturgy, and my lower middle class economics. They have helped me to see that being a Christian means taking seriously what Jesus took seriously. What Jesus took seriously was not believer's baptism by immersion, congregational church government, the priesthood of all believers, and the symbolic view of the ordinances. I do think that Jesus took voluntarism seriously, but what Jesus took really seriously was including the excluded, healing human hurts, confronting the exploiters, sharing what you have, living a life anchored in and under God, and being obedient to that God even in the face of death. It is much easier to be a Baptist than it is to take Jesus seriously.

I have walked much closer to the Baptist ideals than to the Jesus ideals. But those "people, institutions, books, human hurts and joys, good jobs, Holy Scriptures, and Holy Spirit" have been successful enough that I hardly ever brag on being a Baptist anymore. But while I seldom brag, I cannot forget. To some small degree Baptists have set me free, but they have not set me adrift. As long as I can find a Baptist church that will take me and one that I can take, I'll be a Baptist. Their acceptance of me and my stewardship to them is part of the covenant. If they or I ever break that covenant, I'll pack up and move out. But I could never move on without packing some Baptist stuff—golden Baptist stuff—to carry with me.

I would pack "memories," especially memories of relationships with people of the Second Baptist Church in Greenville, Mississippi; First Baptist Church in Ruston, Louisiana; St. Charles Avenue Baptist Church in New Orleans, Louisiana; First Baptist Church in Jefferson City, Tennessee; Crescent Hill Baptist Church in Louisville, Kentucky; and First Baptist Church in Macon, Georgia. And I would pack one other thing. I would pack several extra portions of voluntarism, for I think it is not only essential to good religion but also necessary to being fully human.

But I'm not packing—yet.

Notes

[1]If you want evidence of the socioeconomic stratification of Christian denominations, visit church parking lots on a Sunday morning at 11: 30 and do a quick survey of the vehicles. You will not find many pickups or Chevrolets at the Episcopal church or many Cadillacs or Lexuses at the Pentecostal churches. You can notice something of the same difference, though maybe not as great, if you compare the parking lots of First Baptist Church and Second Baptist Church in the average size town in the South.

[2]To tell the historical story accurately, one has to acknowledge that not all Baptists, even from their beginning, came from the lower strata of society. The phenomenal progress of Baptists on the American frontier and especially in the rural South has left a sociological imprint on Baptists in America, especially in the South. W. W. Sweet's once popular historical treatment of Baptists and the importance of the frontier Baptist preacher intensified this portrayal. See his *Religion on the American Frontier: The Baptists, 1783-1830* (New York: Cooper Square Publishers, Inc., 1964). But as E. Brooks Holifield demonstrated in *The Gentleman Theologians: American Theology in Southern Culture, 1795-1860* (Durham NC: Duke University Press, 1978), Sweet's depiction is not the whole picture.

[3]Langdon Gilkey, "The Threshold of a New Common Freedom," *Criterion* (Divinity School, University of Chicago)37:3 (Autumn 1998) 19.

A Personal Journey to England and Back Again

—— *Cecil P. Staton, Jr.* ——

Like most people who belong to the Baptist clan, I do so for many reasons. I cannot deny that chief among them is the fact that I am Baptist born and Baptist bred. It is not too much to say that it would be almost impossible for me to be anything other than a Baptist. By accident of birth or by divine providence, I was born into a Baptist family living in Greenville, South Carolina, the buckle of the Bible Belt, on January 26, 1958. My birth marked the beginning of another generation in the line of a conspicuous Baptist pedigree. My parents, grandparents, and great-grandparents were all Baptists.

Of course, the Baptist church played a large role in my childhood upbringing. As the old song goes, "It began on the morn of the day that I was born, when the cradle roll added my name." The cradle roll, of course, was the nursery of the local Baptist church. Although my father did not attend church regularly, my mother, Shirley Hughes Staton, was and is a devoted churchwoman. She saw to it that my sister and I were in church every time the doors were opened.

This included a regular mix of Sunday School, preaching services, Training Union, evening services, and Wednesday prayer meetings, not to mention revivals, Bible conferences, evangelism emphases, and Vacation Bible Schools. During the early years of my childhood, church was a place where I found comfort and acceptance. I saw my grandparents there, and they played a large role in my spiritual upbringing. The Baptist church was a place of warm embraces. It was my community, my extended family, a nurturing and gracious environment.

At the tender age of eight (1966) a Billy Graham crusade came to Greenville, and I attended each service with my family. There I felt the urge to commit my life to Christ. As the choir sang, "Just as I am, without one plea," I moved forward to act upon that urge. The next Sunday I "walked the aisle" and professed my faith before the Brandon Baptist Church where I was later baptized.

Some time afterward my family moved to the Washington Avenue Baptist Church whose motto was "the end of your search for a gospel church." The pastor was Dr. W. Daniel Greer, and the minister of music was Claude Turner. These men exercised enormous influence upon my life in my adolescent and teenage years. Washington Avenue was a warm and welcoming place. The music was emotionally stirring, and the preaching was lively. Every service ended with an invitation for the lost to come to Jesus and the backslidden to return to the fold.

There we had regular doses of famous Baptist preachers and evangelists: J. Harold Smith, Eddie Lieberman, Hyman Appleman, Vance Havner, and Eddie Martin were all regulars in a rotation of evangelistic fervor and earnest study of the Scriptures. We baptized frequently, prayed often, preached with all one's might, and sang up a storm. This was conservative Baptist life in the sixties and seventies. We loved Jesus, believed the Bible, and wanted everyone to get saved and join our fellowship. We were big, with more than 1,000 persons attending Sunday School every week. Our services were broadcast on radio and television. We were growing, and we were proud. There was nothing better than to be a Southern Baptist.

Our missionary house was almost always filled with a missionary family on furlough, having returned to the States from some distant land. We often heard stories about how the heathens were being saved. We learned of exotic countries far away and the bizarre customs of people who did not know our Jesus. The offerings were big, and the commitment was genuine. The world must be won to our Jesus, and the way to do it was through the Cooperative Program. We were Baptists, we were good, and we were winning the world for Christ.

In this context I was embraced and affirmed. I felt special and needed. Perhaps God could use me as He used Dr. Greer, Claude Turner, and the missionaries. Opportunities for leadership arose, and I was as active in church as a teenager could be. I was not a normal teenager. I did not listen to rock-'n'-roll music. I was comfortable with the old Baptist maxim: "I don't drink, I don't smoke, I don't chew, and I don't go with girls that do."

One day a guest preacher gave the invitation for all who would give their lives to the service of Christ to come forward. I did, and dedicated my life to full-time Christian service. For me the greatest gift, and the one I hoped I would be given by God, was the gift of preaching.

In due course I became a child-prodigy preacher. I was licensed to preach at age seventeen and ordained at age nineteen. Washington Avenue had a large children's church that met separately each Sunday. I became the pastor of that church, speaking each week to as many as 200 children and workers. Baptisms increased. Soon invitations came to preach in other churches, and I received regular invitations to preach revivals.

Then the time came to prepare more formally for Christian service. I knew that it was important to have a college and seminary degree. Fortunately, my mother preached education and expected me to go to college. Education brought respect and opened doors. I had no idea at the time, however, how a preacher might benefit from college and seminary.

Furman University was in my hometown, was a Baptist school, and seemed the obvious choice. Working part-time at a "Christian" radio station in Travelers Rest, South Carolina, I had the occasion to meet Jim Pitts, associate chaplain at Furman, on the backlot of a circus. Jim, a circus aficionado, was promoting the event, and the radio station had been enlisted to drum up a crowd. In the bright yellow remote broadcast van, I interviewed whomever Jim could rustle up from the circus sideshow. How Baptist can you get!

With Jim Pitts' help I made my way to Furman University, and there encountered Baptist saints such as L. D. Johnson, Theron Price, and T. C. Smith. I was warned by my pastor, "Don't let them ruin you." I did not really understand what he meant. Although I had never met a supposed liberal Baptist, I had been warned by some evangelists that there were so-called Christians who did not use the King James Version, or even worse, did not believe the Bible. Meanwhile, Washington Avenue invited me to join the staff of the church as Minister of Evangelism.

My pastor had every reason to be concerned. Furman was a life-changing experience. My academic career was not launched without difficulty. Eventually, I was referred to by the religion faculty as a "late bloomer." But bloom I did. Furman showed me another side of Baptist life. There I discovered that it was possible to love God with the mind as well as with the heart and soul. Washington Avenue was good with the heart and soul. Furman gave me a love for the life of the mind. There I grew to appreciate the gift of teaching and dared to dream that I could one day be as good a teacher as my Furman mentors. There and at the First Baptist Church of Greenville, I heard a different kind of preaching that touched my mind along with my heart. At the end of my four years I was off to seminary with Furman's blessing, having received the Baggott Award as the outstanding religion major of the class of 1980.

I arrived on the campus of Southeastern Baptist Theological Seminary in late August 1980. Southern Baptists had just elected the second in a series of fundamentalist presidents, a trend that continues until today. Few, if any, of us knew or understood what this would mean for our preparation and ministry. I began my journey with a generation of Baptist seminary students who have known nothing but controversy throughout their entire careers. I received the M.Div. degree in December 1992 and the Th.M. degree in December 1985. By that time we had become worried.

Prior to President Randall Lolley's departure in 1988, Southeastern Baptist Theological Seminary was a remarkable center for theological education, perhaps the best Southern Baptists have ever created. The quality of the faculty and the curriculum was known literally around the world. It was good enough that I could gain acceptance into the doctoral program of the University of Oxford in 1985. My mentors sent me off to Oxford with the hope and anticipation that I would return to teach at a Southern Baptist seminary or college.

I look back upon those years with deep gratitude and joy. I was never more proud to be a Baptist. Southeastern afforded me an appropriate mix of experiences for the heart, soul, and mind. I never regretted attending Southeastern for a moment; it prepared me well for my goal of attaining a Doctor of Philosophy degree in Old Testament and Hebrew. My mentors, including Dr. John I Durham and Dr. B. Elmo Scoggin, were Christian gentlemen who were committed to their students and proud of Southeastern and its contribution to Baptist life. Perhaps the saddest result of the controversy for me was the loss of this great tradition.

In September 1985, I boarded a plane for England to begin my years as a student at the ancient University of Oxford. I had never been to England. All I had to guide me were impressions from movies, books, and the reflections of the people I knew who had been there before me. I had the privilege of being a member of Regent's Park College, one of only two free-church institutions affiliated with the University. Regent's Park had begun as a theological college for the preparation of Baptist ministers in the late eighteenth century. Through the good work of famous Old Testament scholar and principal H. Wheeler Robinson, Regent's had become a more formal part of the University in the 1940s.

At Regent's Park I had the privilege of living in a Baptist community in a country with a state religion, Anglicanism. It was there that I really learned for the first time the significance of our Baptist heritage and its principles. I had read about them, and I had been taught about them. I thought I understood our cherished principles, but there they came alive. Unlike the southern United States where I grew up and lived, Baptists were in the minority in England. Out of a population of approximately 55 million, there are fewer than 100,000 Baptists in the United Kingdom. In Oxford my wife and I were members of the New Road Baptist Church, which could trace its history back to the seventeenth century. We dined in Helwys Hall at Regent's Park, named for Thomas Helwys, the early seventeenth-century pioneer of religious liberty. In the Regent's Angus Library I could hold in my hands one of only two extant copies of Helwys' classic statement on religious liberty, *A Short Declaration of the Mystery of Iniquity*. The only other copy, containing the original inscription to King James, is in the Bodleian Library at Oxford. The inscription reads:

> Hear, O king, and despise not the counsel of the poor, and let their complaints come before thee. The king is a mortal man and not God, therefore has no power over the immortal souls of his subjects, to make laws and ordinances for them, and to set spiritual lords over them. If the king has authority to make spiritual lords and laws, then he is an immortal God and not a mortal man. O king, be not seduced by your poor subjects who ought and will obey you in all things with body, life, and goods, or else let their lives be taken from the earth. God save the king.[1]

Many assume that this inscription sealed Helwys' fate. Following his arrest in 1612 he was placed in Newgate Prison, where he later died.

In England I learned what it means to be Baptist by conviction and not merely by accident of birth or by the ease of the majority. In the UK being Baptist often carries a large price. Most Baptists and their churches reflect humble origins and means. They have never known the privilege of being the majority. They do not know what it is to have political power or financial security. The Baptists I encountered in those critical years helped me enormously to value my religious heritage and to make it my own. I returned to the United States in August 1988, more of a Baptist than when I had left.

Although I had conversations with Dr. Morris Ashcraft, Dean of Southeastern Seminary, about the possibilities of teaching there, the resignation of Ashcraft and Lolley in 1987 put an end to that dream. When I returned to the States in August 1988, with an Oxford D.Phil. in hand, I did not have a job.

Several interviews at Baptist institutions led me to the conclusion that I was considered too "Baptist" for schools that had already made the break with Southern Baptists. Their freedom was taking them in new and different directions. And I was too liberal, or at least too suspect, for those that had not yet or could not break away. Furman, Southeastern, and Oxford were a potent mix that spelled "liberal" for the cautious.

Dr. Jim Pitts, chaplain at Furman, came to my rescue again by introducing me to Dr. Alan Gragg, Vice President for Academic Affairs at Brewton-Parker College in Mount Vernon, Georgia. I was fortunate to teach at that institution from January 1989 until I left to be the first full-time president and publisher of Smyth & Helwys and publisher of Mercer University Press in the summer of 1991.

Since returning to the United States in 1988, I have questioned on several occasions whether I should remain a member of a Baptist church. Many friends from my seminary years, particularly women, made the choice long ago to find their spiritual homes in other communities of faith. Even today I find that I am embarrassed when I must say, "I am a Baptist." The name is tarnished. Certainly it means more than arrogance and ignorance. I feel like I need to take out some silver polish and give it a working over so that the shine can come through once again. I am convinced that underneath the discoloration lies something of enormous value for the Christian witness.

My work today with Smyth & Helwys and Mercer University helps me to remain a Baptist. I am confident that I will always remain committed to the "Baptist Vision," even though I have concluded that the Southern Baptist Convention, so dominant in the South, is no longer my spiritual home. Ultimately I am committed to the baptistic way, not a denominational entity. It may be some time before the word Baptist can be rescued from the tarnish that has overcome it. I am convinced, however, that Baptist principles will never be completely destroyed. I have dedicated my life for the past eight years to reclaiming the Baptist heritage through publishing and to rescuing it from the results of twenty years of controversy.

In conclusion, I am like many others in this book. I am Baptist for many reasons. Given my pilgrimage, I could not help but be Baptist. It is my birthright and, like every family, belonging brings joys, heartaches, headaches, and great promise.

Someone has said you can choose your friends, but not your family. I suppose I could choose not to be a member of a Baptist church, but I do not ever think I could stop being Baptist. When you are Baptist born and Baptist bred, it is hard to get Baptist out of your blood. Having gone to England, the land of John Smyth and Thomas Helwys, and back, being Baptist is for me a life-changing commitment. Being Baptist is about embracing what ultimately matters, a warm and comforting family of faith, a Bible to live by, a heart filled with the love of Christ, a desire to share the good news, and the ambiguity of freedom and responsibility in Christ. This wonderful combination comprises a unique spiritual heritage that has everything to do with why I remain a Baptist.

Note

[1]Thomas Helwys, *A Short Declaration of the Mystery of Iniquity*, Richard Groves, ed. (Macon GA: Mercer University Press, 1998).

A Baptist Missionary Pilgrimage

Charles Frank "T" Thomas

As many others have written, I am tempted to say, "I am a Baptist because my parents were Baptists." To say such a thing, however, would be a little ironic in that I have spent the majority of my adult life overseas, sharing the gospel with folks who might likewise say, "I'm Catholic (or Orthodox or Muslim or Animistic) because my parents were." Surely there must be more at work here than a hereditary understanding of God—and there is!

I am a Baptist today because of the spiritual pilgrimage the Lord has led me on during the last forty or so years. It is a voyage that began in the suburbs of Atlanta and has led from my native Georgia to parts of the Southeast and then on to Africa and Europe. This journey has been marked by a number of people and experiences that have enriched my understanding of the Creator and His love for me. It has been essentially a Baptist pilgrimage, and I would like to share with you a few thoughts from that journey.

Baptist Family

As Paul said concerning Timothy's family, I am reminded of the faith that dwelled first in my grandmother and then in my mother. "Mama Mac," my maternal grandmother, was a committed Christian. Some of my first memories are of her sitting in a rocking chair and reading God's Word for hours on end. She came from a long line of Baptists and loved her little country church in rural Georgia. She never picked up the Bible without washing her hands and would scold me if I set anything on top of it. When I asked her about these seemingly strange practices, she replied fervently, "Well, it is the Almighty's book!"

However, it was my mother who was the earliest and most important Baptist influence on my life. Mom said she first took me to church when I was three weeks old, though I don't remember it. I do remember sitting in church with her in the days before we had extended session. When I began to squirm during the service, she gave me a "holy pinch" that calmed things down—at least for a while.

In my early years Mom always took me to church with a nickel in one hand for the offering and a penny in the other for the missionaries. She saw to it that I went to Sunday School, Training Union, Choir, and Sunbeams each week, and later to Royal Ambassadors. In fact, most of the Scriptures I know by heart, I learned in RAs.

Mother taught the "old ladies" Sunday School class, as she called it, until she became one of them herself. The "Circle" was the center of her social life. She would rather have missed the worship service than her circle meeting! She loved missions, prayed aloud everyday for the missionaries, and always asked the Lord to call out more to work in his fields.

The day my wife and I told my mother we were applying for foreign missionary service, I was surprised at her reaction. She said, "Oh no! Not you! You can't take the grandchildren overseas!" Shocked, I replied, "But mother, you always have prayed for God to send out more missionaries." Her response was, "Yes, but I never meant *you*!" Quickly, though, she adjusted to the idea and spent her last twenty-four years bragging to everyone about her missionary son and family.

Carolyn McIntosh (Thomas) was a lady of high principles and moral integrity who taught me a great deal through her example. She rarely missed work and had more than six months of sick leave accumulated when she retired. She was never late for a meeting and believed that "on time" meant being early. But most importantly, she encouraged me to do the best with what God had given me.

Baptist Friends

As I went from grade school to high school, the Lord watched over and kept me from getting into trouble. A dear high school counselor gently directed me to a small Baptist college in Greenville, South Carolina, rather than to the University of Georgia where most of my friends had enrolled. Furman University proved to be a true turning point in my life, as it was there that I met my future wife.

I saw Kathie Brown my first day on campus, in the registration line. It would be nice to say that I was first attracted to her for spiritual reasons, but that was not initially the case; those were, after all, the mini-skirted sixties. We were married two years later as we discovered that we had a common interest in each other and in foreign missionary service. Kathie has a rich Baptist heritage. Her father and grandfather were both Baptist preachers, and her aunt and uncle were missionaries in China.

During those four years at Furman I received a balanced but strong Baptist influence from L. D. Johnson, Jim Pitts, and a seminary-quality religion department headed by Theron Price. It was, in fact, Dr. Price who encouraged me not to attend Princeton divinity school as I had intended, but to go to a Southern Baptist seminary if I really wanted to pursue missions with the Foreign Mission Board. Following graduation Kathie and I and our two-month-old baby set off for Southern Seminary in Louisville, Kentucky. I later completed my seminary training at Southeastern Seminary in Wake Forest, North Carolina. Luther Copeland was a great influence, and his stories from the mission field continued to fan the flames of our call. Only years later did I understood what he meant when he said, "On the mission field you become more 'Baptistic' and more ecumenical at the same time."

Baptist Missionary

Upon completion of seminary we were accepted for missionary service in a French-speaking country in West Africa. In December 1974 we moved to France to study French in preparation for work in Ouagadougou, Upper Volta (or Burkina Faso, as it is called now.) Though our stay in Africa was cut short due to a health problem with one of our children, we were confronted with a distinctly hostile and pagan culture. We found ourselves on the front lines of evangelism, sharing the gospel with people who had neither seen a Bible nor heard the name of Jesus.

The few Christians, especially the Baptists we encountered in Upper Volta, were those who had found the gospel to be genuinely "good news" for them. We were witnesses to several events that some would call miracles, but that the African Christians viewed as normal everyday occurrences. Let me share one of those events with you.

Along with another Baptist missionary and a local evangelist, we had been doing "vivals" (there was nothing to "re," so we didn't call them "revivals") in a number of villages. The Lord had been blessing, and we had seen hundreds come to faith in Jesus Christ. However, in one village we had seen almost no results after three or four days of witnessing and evangelistic services. The older missionary suggested a day of prayer and fasting to ask God to begin to move in a mighty way.

The next morning we found an isolated spot and began to pray. By early afternoon I felt compelled to preach to the elders, who were drinking beer under a tree not far from us. My colleague said, "But who will translate into the local dialect if you preach to them?" I said I didn't know, but that God was urging me to go and share a word with them. The other missionary said he would continue to pray while I went.

On my way to speak with the elders our translator returned from another village and offered to help. I shared John 3:18 and told the men that the Lord was calling them that day to salvation, that they must choose either to continue in their sinful ways or to accept the gift of eternal life in Jesus Christ. I emphasized the fact that if they continued as before, God said they were already condemned.

At that moment they began pointing at an enormous bush fire several hundred yards away. I said, "See! God has given you a sign. Repent and live eternally with Him, or remain as you are under condemnation." I put my Bible down beside their pot of beer and returned to the place where the other missionary was praying.

When we got there he asked how it had gone. I said that since the Lord had sent the fire at just the right moment, it had gone fine. My friend asked, "What fire?" The translator and I both said that he couldn't have missed it since it was in his direction. He said, "Show me!" We started off walking that way. We went a mile or more but saw no burned grass or other evidence of a fire. Yet that night a large portion of the village gave their hearts to Christ. My African Christian friends find this story very ordinary, as the mighty works of God for them are not confined to the pages of the Bible.

All but two of our twenty-five years of missionary service have been spent in France. Unlike the Bible Belt of the USA, Kathie and I discovered a country with the outward trappings of Christianity, but only a small community of faith. Francis Schaffer said that people in Western Europe have been immunized with just enough Christianity to keep them immune from the real thing. Baptists—who number less than 10,000 in a country of 60,000,000—are less well known than Jehovah's Witnesses or Mormons in the US. In starting churches in France, we have discovered what life as a small, misunderstood, and sometimes persecuted minority is like. Yet, the Baptists of France have a vibrant and energetic faith. We have learned from worshiping with these committed Christians what it means to take a significant stand for one's faith in front of family and friends and in the workplace.

I remember a church member in our mission in Toulouse who lost his job because he refused to cheat on his tax calculations at his boss' request. He stood up during the Sunday morning service and proclaimed that the Lord would not let his family suffer for his act of faith. Despite the economic slowdown at the time, he found a new job the following day and of course gave all the credit to the Lord.

On another occasion in a mission church we had begun in the southern suburbs of Paris, a converted Muslim lady brought her son to a midweek Bible and prayer service. Mohammed (not his real name) was about eighteen and had a rather severe vision problem. During our prayer time a zealous deacon prayed aloud for him, saying, "Dear Lord, you brought Mohammed here tonight. He cannot see well, but we ask you to open his spiritual eyes as well as his physical eyes so that he can see you now!" When Mohammed opened his eyes, he could indeed see again. A short time later he accepted Christ and was baptized. Soon afterward he returned to his home country of Algeria, where he led others to faith in Christ and started an underground church. Those are the types of Baptists we have been privileged to work with and to learn from in France.

French worship services are joyful occasions with as much as an hour for praise and singing. The Lord's Supper is celebrated every Sunday and is often used as a time of invitation. Positioned in the middle of the service, it serves as the centerpiece of worship. Baptism in France tends to come at a later age—sixteen is the youngest—and candidates always testify in the service before being baptized. While these traditions and practices seem a bit strange, the result is a vibrant and dynamic faith that put Baptists on the cutting edge of the evangelical movement in France and Europe.

When the Berlin wall and communism fell in Eastern Europe in 1989–1990, we were asked to transfer to Romania. In Bucharest we started a church while teaching at the seminary and introducing Master Life to the churches there. We met an incredible Baptist, Dr. Ion Bunaciu. During the communist days in Romania he was pastor of the Providence Baptist Church in Bucharest and president of the Baptist seminary. He is the author of more than a dozen books, including *The History of Baptists in Romania as I Lived It*, in which he denounces the compromises of some and praises the courage of others during the dark years of that country's history.

One day a delegation from another Baptist school visited at the seminary to persuade the faculty to sign the Chicago Statement on Inerrancy. Dr. Bunaciu was furious and stated flatly that he would not do so. "Are we not able to write our own confession of faith? Do we need non-Baptists and foreigners to write for us?" he proclaimed. The faculty voted unanimously not to sign the statement! The Romanian Baptist confession of faith speaks of the Bible as the spring from which truth is revealed to humankind. I regard this as a much more beautiful term than "inerrancy," which does not even exist in the Romanian language.

During our years of missionary service my wife's father was a gentle but powerful influence on me. Rev. Thomas R. Brown, or "Papa," as we called him, gradually filled the void left by my own father's death nearly thirty years earlier. Though he never dominated, he loved and encouraged me like a son. Most importantly, he taught me what it means to stand up for what is right even if the cost is great.

His wise counsel helped Kathie and me through our decision to resign from the Foreign Mission Board in 1992, even though we had two daughters in college and three younger ones still at home. During that difficult moment he said, "There comes a time once or twice in a Christian's life when they have an opportunity to do something great for God. These actions always require courage and sometimes sacrifice." While others told us we were crazy to leave the FMB in protest over the fundamentalist takeover of the Board, Rev. Brown said, "just do the right thing." We followed his advice and in May 1992 left Romania and missionary service to return to the USA. Despite our grief and pain at leaving a life we felt called to, we have never regretted doing what we felt was the right thing.

Baptist with a Big "B"

For the last six years we have worked with the Cooperative Baptist Fellowship, continuing to share the gospel overseas. The Lord has given us a new Baptist family and a renewed vision for sharing the Good News with those who have been the most neglected by conventional missionary activity, or "World A," as we say at CBF. These changes have made us stronger Christians and reinforced our Baptist identity.

Though we are first and foremost Christians, we also are strongly attached to that particular family of evangelicals worldwide known as Baptists. As a Brazilian missionary with whom we worked in France used to say, "I am Baptist with a big 'B'!" During a number of years leading up to 1992, I was at times ashamed to say that I was a Baptist. Since joining CBF, however, I have found a renewed pride in my heritage and spiritual family.

Perhaps the most defining moment in my Baptist pilgrimage came during a conference in Switzerland a number of years ago. John David Hopper led a group of Americans on a walking tour of Zurich, and I tagged along. At one point we stopped on an old stone bridge where John David explained that on that very spot Anabaptists were drowned rather than recant their faith and firm conviction in believer's baptism. I was reminded in an indelible way that we are but a part of a long line of faithful followers of Christ who have suffered more often than not for their Baptist beliefs.

So, it has been more than a particular upbringing or the result of certain struggles in the USA that have made me the Baptist I am today. The witness and testimony of overseas Baptists have further shaped my identity. As Dr. Copeland foretold, this has made me more "Baptistic" and also more thankful for all God is doing in Christian groups around the world.

A Way of Being Christian
Daniel Vestal

Several years ago I took a mission trip outside the United States. In a casual conversation a young man asked me what I believed about God. Part of my response was, "I am Christian." As the conversation progressed, it became clear that the word "Christian" has all kinds of implications. In certain countries it is a cultural designation or one describing ethnic origin. In America it has political connotations or is associated with all sorts of sentimental and romantic notions. Yet the term is a good one and one worth preserving.

In a similar way the term Baptist has been so corrupted and caricatured that many would rather not use it at all. But I can still say, "I am a Baptist," not just by birth or convenience, but by conscience and conviction. Being Baptist helps define who I am and what I believe.

For me, being a Baptist is a way of being Christian. This is not to imply that only Baptists are Christians—although I've known some Baptists who've acted like that's what they believed. Anyone who confesses that Jesus is Lord is to me a Christian brother or sister and a part of the mystical body of Christ. The church is made up of many parts "and no one can say 'Jesus is Lord' except by the Holy Spirit" (1 Cor 12:3). Within this mystical body we belong to each other, and we benefit from the contribution that each brings to it.

Speaking historically and theologically, we describe the church as orthodox, catholic, reformed, evangelical, ecumenical, and charismatic. Each of these designations defines an important and biblical characteristic of the church as a whole and as Christians individually. In the truest sense I am orthodox, catholic, reformed, evangelical, ecumenical, and charismatic.

To say "I am Baptist" also is to confess some important and biblical characteristics of what it means to be a Christian. To be perfectly honest, these characteristics have not been articulated and championed by Baptists alone. But for almost 400 years folks who were given the designation "Baptist" have borne witness—sometimes at great price—to truths that for me are defining what it means to be a Christian. What are those truths?

First, relationship to God must be personal and voluntary. Faith in Jesus Christ as Savior and Lord is the result of free choice. No one can choose for me, and I cannot choose for anyone else. Coercion by civil authorities or ecclesiastical authorities cannot create faith. Baptism is for believers only because it is a public confession resulting from a personal and voluntary decision. Of course, personal choice and voluntary decision are the result of God's grace and response to the Holy Spirit's initiative, but each of us is free and competent to make such a response and to accept or refuse grace. This basic and fundamental idea has not always been accepted, however. I am a Baptist because, for me, being a Christian means having a personal and voluntary relationship with God through faith in Jesus Christ.

Also, I am a Baptist because being a Christian means that I grow in that relationship though personal Scripture study and prayer. The Bible is the written Word of God, and I need to understand and receive its truth for my life. The good news is that I can interpret its meaning, discern its message, and apply its precepts. I don't have to submit to someone else's interpretation or subordinate myself to someone else's discernment or application. I can study the Scriptures for myself and be informed and formed by them. Of course, the freedom, privilege, and responsibility for personal Scripture study is useless without the divine work of the Holy Spirit. And if I am serious about learning and growing in faith, I must be attentive to the witness of other Christians as they listen to Scripture. It is also possible for me to misinterpret and misapply the Bible. But, if I am to grow in my relationship to God, I must humbly yet confidently open the Scriptures to receive truth for myself.

I also must pray, directly to God without human intermediary or human institution. I must speak *and* listen to the Eternal Thou. No pope, council, convention, pastor, or preacher need tell me how or what to pray. In the Old Testament the priests of Israel were privileged to offer sacrifices and represent the people in a holy place. But now I myself am a priest, able to commune and communicate with the Holy. And my priesthood before God is not dependent upon my status in society, my economic condition, or my educational level. Rather, it is secured for me by God's creation of me and Christ's sacrificial death for me. These radical ideas, rooted in Scripture, have been championed by Baptists.

A Way of Doing Church

Being a Baptist is also a way of doing church, that is, a way of functioning in a community of faith and living in relationship with other Christians. For Baptists, a congregation is a people gathered voluntarily and willingly. Each individual belongs because of personal faith in Jesus Christ confessed openly and publicly in believer's baptism. Church is a fellowship of individuals who have freely covenanted themselves into relationship with each other. No one inducts another into the fellowship or incorporates them by proxy. Each enters personally and individually.

When individuals enter, they see themselves as "members of the body" or "living stones being built into a spiritual house" or a "holy priesthood." Each person is responsible for the life of the fellowship, discerning of the will of God for the fellowship, the health and welfare of the fellowship, and ministry in the fellowship. Understood in this light, no hierarchy should be visible. Within the church, first- and second-class membership is unacceptable. There are diversity of gifts and variety of functions, but no pyramid of authority or importance. All are ministers, all are servants, and all are witnesses.

In a Baptist vision of church, the freedom of each individual is treasured and cherished. Indeed, an authentic belief in freedom and a willingness to live with the consequences and even the confusion of that freedom is one of the distinguishing characteristics of a Baptist. Freedom will inevitably result in diversity, not enforced conformity. There will be doctrinal differences, even within a church, along with differences resulting from ethical choices. Those differences may lead to discussion and debate, but debate is not necessarily bad. It can be dialogue where greater understanding of truth is the result. What is bad is when discussion and debate lead to exclusion and division.

In a Baptist vision of church, each person is free and responsible to make doctrinal and ethical choices. But each is also free and responsible to love those whose doctrinal and ethical decisions differ from their own. Let me be specific: I am not a sacramentalist, but I must respect and love the sacramentalist who in freedom has come to such a conviction. I am not a Calvinist, but I must respect and love the Calvinist who in freedom has come to such a conviction. Galatians 5:13-14 says it clearly,

> You, my brothers, were called to be free, but do not use your freedom to indulge in sinful nature. Rather, serve one another in love. The entire law is summed up in a single command, Love your neighbor as yourself.

Baptists have deep theological convictions but also recognize the one who differs as one to be loved and even to be served.

In a Baptist vision of church, the *episkopos* (clergy leaders) and *presbuteros* (lay leaders) are not superior to the *laos* (the people). They do not make decisions and pass them on. Rather, they lead by humbly serving and helping each person to discover his/her giftedness and then strengthening the unity of the fellowship for congregational decision making.

In a Baptist vision of church, men and women are equal. Because of Christ there is no male or female, just as there is no Jew or Greek, slave or free. Participation and leadership in the church are not determined by gender, social status, or economic condition; these are determined by the grace and call of God. Likewise, there is no special class or office that can exclusively minister grace to the whole of the church. Each can minister grace, and all should minister grace. Not just a few are ordained by God to evangelize, baptize, and administer the sacraments.

In a Baptist vision of church, the Holy Spirit communes with and communicates to each member and to all members, resulting in a shared life and vision. The Baptist way of doing church is not easy, and it can be messy and very inefficient. But when a family of faith lives in mutual submission, gentleness, and patience, the result is glorious.

A Way of Living in the World

Finally, being Baptist is a way of confronting culture, interacting with society, and relating to people, that is, a way of living in the world. For Baptists, an individual Christian and a congregation of Christians are to be in the world but not be of the world. We are clearly commissioned to go into the world as witnesses, servants, and ministers.

Baptists are a missionary people. We believe that the good news of Jesus Christ is for all cultures and nations. Every individual on earth is born with the need and capacity for a personal relationship with God, and every individual is guilty of sin before God. Jesus Christ is Lord and the world's only Savior. So our privilege and responsibility is to call all people to faith in Christ and to a relationship with God through Christ. But our missionary task is to be fulfilled by recognizing and respecting the freedom of every individual either to accept or to reject Christ. We do not use force, coercion, or intimidation to bring about conversion. We appeal to people's conscience and seek to persuade them, but we never use the power of the sword or the state to bring about faith.

Baptists are a people committed to social justice. We believe Christians should be like light, salt, and leaven in society, influencing and transforming it. We believe the church should be both prophetic and priestly. We are to cry out against injustices, be peacemakers, and work for reconciliation. This means that Christians should and will be involved in politics, government, and other public roles of influence. We must act publicly and privately, respecting the freedom of every person's conscience. We will not seek to mandate Christian convictions or behavior through coercive laws. We will not use the power of the state to force religious conformity or religious devotion. Rather, we will seek social justice the same way we seek individual conversion: through prayer, persuasion, and the personal example of Christian character.

Baptists are a servant people, seeking to minister grace, healing, and help to those in need. Our posture in society is to be that of humble caregivers, good Samaritans, and suffering servants. Our concern should always be for the poor, the powerless, and the disenfranchised. We are called upon to give without expecting anything in return, to seek the kingdom of God more than any earthly kingdom, to practice love and not hate, and to work tirelessly for the peace and brotherhood of all nations.

Recently I received a letter from an older pastor saying, "I'm a Christian by conversion and a Baptist by conviction." That says it well. Having received grace and having experienced the reality of Jesus Christ, I have struggled to discern what that means and how to live it in the church and in the world. I have been aided and assisted by biblical revelation, the indwelling Spirit, and a great "cloud of witnesses" down through the ages. The results of that struggle are some convictions and commitments. For me, the best way of defining and describing these convictions is to confess, "I am a Baptist."

A Baptist Kind of Christian
─────── *Charles R. Wade* ───────

The easy answer to any question about why I am anything at all is: "My parents, J. W. and Nellie Jean Wade." I guess this answer applies also to the question of why I am a Baptist. I remember long talks with my preacher father, who eagerly shared the good news of Christ with anyone who crossed his path. He was glad, even proud, to be a Baptist kind of Christian. He taught me why Baptists believed as we did by citing Scripture that he felt clearly showed the way to where we were. I had the feeling that the Bible was an old but new book; that Paul and Silas had done their missionary work not so very long ago; that the Calvary Baptist Church of Durant and the Nogales Avenue Baptist Church of Tulsa, Oklahoma, were just barely removed from the New Testament churches in Ephesus, Philippi, and Rome . . . we were kissin' cousins! I was glad to be a Baptist kind of Christian, as I recall, for these reasons:

- We believed that Jesus really could save anyone from sin, hell, and the grave.

- We believed that a person who had received such a gift should live like it. Gratitude for salvation caused one to want to be obedient to God and to encourage others to believe by the sincerity of one's faith and the character of one's life.

- We believed that the Bible was true and sufficient to lead us to salvation. God spoke to us out of these pages. We believed that these words were inspired by God's heart and recorded by men who knew and trusted God. We could trust the guidance, promises, warnings, and comforts of this book.

- We believed that music should move our hearts to joy, repentance, and serious reflection about being willing to go "Wherever He Leads."

- We believed that the Bible should be preached with conviction and power, not quietly or timidly, that the pulpit from which the full counsel of God was preached should be front and center in the auditorium so that no one could miss the fact that "the preaching of the cross is to them that perish foolishness; but unto us which are saved it is the power of God" (1 Cor 1:18 KJV).

- We believed in praying earnestly for people who needed to be saved. Every invitation at the close of the sermon for people to come to Christ was a terrible and wonderful moment. Some would turn and go away, but others would open their lives in repentance and faith to the love of God.

- We believed that God loved everyone and called everyone we knew, at least, to be saved. But we also respected their right to say, "No." We believed in every person's God-given freedom to believe or not to believe. I can hear my father say, "I would do anything I could to help you believe, but I would not raise one finger to force you to Christ. Indeed, though I might disagree with everything you say, I would give my life to defend your freedom to believe and choose as you will."

- We believed that no one stood between the individual believer and God. Jesus was the "only mediator" we needed or that God had provided. Therefore, the Lord's Supper was passed to the believers. We didn't have to go forward and kneel before anyone to receive what Jesus had given to us. He had invited us to his table!

- We believed that no one could decide religious faith for another; everyone had to believe for themselves and, therefore, no one but believers were ready for baptism. Children could be baptized, but first they had to be old enough (the age of accountability) to acknowledge that they had sinned against God and needed the death of Jesus Christ to forgive and cleanse their sins. In genuine sorrow for sin and glad thankfulness for God's love expressed in Jesus' sacrifice, anyone —boy or girl, man or woman—could step forward and into God's salvation.

Growing up in that environment, I felt accepted and loved. But I also felt challenged to be everything God wanted me to be. There was no excuse for laziness, carelessness, or immorality in light of what was at stake: the souls of my friends and the integrity of my character. Would I live up to the calling of Christ in my life?

As a college student, I began to realize the strengths in other Christian communions and began to try to understand more clearly what the options really were for a follower of Christ. But nothing I read, heard, or experienced tempted me away from what I knew as a Baptist.

In seminary I studied Baptist history, and the pride and gratitude I felt for men and women who bravely acted on their convictions moved me to affirm more deeply my Baptist heritage. The gallant early Anabaptists Conrad Grebel, Felix Manz and his mother, Balthasar Hubmaier, all stirred in me a profound admiration.[1] The early English Baptists John Smyth and Thomas Helwys caused me to want to defend religious liberty at all costs. I was personally motivated to greater service by the stories of William Carey, the English Baptist cobbler and the father of the modern mission movement, and of Adoniram and Ann Judson and their friend, Luther Rice, Congregational missionaries who became Baptists as they studied the New Testament on their way to Burma. I became aware of the racial prejudice that marked so deeply the soul of Southern Baptists, and gladly sought to do what I could to help shift the hearts of our people to embrace all of God's people.

In light of all this, how could I be anything other than a Baptist? The churches of my childhood and the churches where I have been pastor since I was fifteen years old have been safe havens and amazingly encouraging fellowships that have believed in me, prayed for me, and loved me.

For the last several years, as I have tried to make the Baptist way plain for people who wanted to join our fellowship, I have found that what is most important and significant to me is this: at our heart is the message of Jesus Christ: "Come, follow me . . . and I will make you fishers of men" (Matt 4:19). The Christian faith is about Jesus Christ: following him, becoming like him, giving one's life in service to others that the world might be saved (20:25-28). The good news is to be shared, not privately held, and so Matthew summarizes and concludes his account of the gospel by hearing Jesus Christ send his church into the world to make disciples, baptizing and teaching them (28:18-20).

Believer's Baptism, the Gift Baptists Bring to the Table

The great sign of God's calling to live in the world "on mission" is baptism. Baptism in the New Testament is the dipping or immersing in water of a new believer in Jesus Christ (see Acts 2:38, 8:26-40, 9:18, 10:47-48, 16:29-34; Rom 6:4).

Baptism gives Baptists their name. The name is a shortened version of Anabaptists, which was first a nickname given to our spiritual forebears as a label expressing disdain and anger. The Anabaptists had recovered an old idea from the New Testament: only believers were proper candidates for baptism.[2] And they defended this conviction at great personal cost, even to persecution and death.

Baptism in New Testament times was first a Jewish rite by which Gentiles could be baptized into the Jewish faith and covenant. When Jesus went to John the Baptist at the Jordan River, John was baptizing Jews as a sign of repentance, cleansing, and a new trust in God (Matt 3:1-12, 13-17; John 3:22-36).

Baptists see truth in the celebration of believer's baptism by immersion that can help to renew the church. It is the gift Baptists gladly bring to the table as Christians sit down to consider how we shall act out our faith in the new millennium. Baptists believe in the importance of baptism for these reasons:

• Baptism is about the gospel of Jesus Christ; his death, burial, and resurrection; the new life he gives to all who believe; the confident hope we have because of his victory over death (Rom 6:4).

• Baptism is about God's call to every believer to be a *servant* disciple (Matt 3:17).

• Baptism is about each individual answering the call to follow Jesus as a personal decision to respond affirmatively to the Holy Spirit's prompting. Baptists do not carry another to baptism; each person has to go there for him/herself (see the Acts references above).

- Baptism is about the freedom of each individual to accept the mark of Christ—baptism. Baptists do not coerce anyone into the water. We do not threaten that unless someone is baptized in our manner, they are not one of Christ's. Nor do we use the powers of government to compel conformity to our doctrine (Matt 22:21; Acts 5:29, 10:47-48, 16:29-34).

- Baptism is about being brought into the church, the body of Christ. This local body of believers baptizes and welcomes us into the family of faith. We become members of the visible church, grafted or transplanted into the community of God's people. This is the work of the Holy Spirit, who was visibly present at Jesus' baptism and is spiritually present at every baptism (Acts 2:41-47; Eph 1:22-23, 2:13-22; Col 2:9-12; John 15:4-5; 1 Cor 12:12-13; Matt 3:16).

Believer's baptism is a clear and visible sign and testimony that the Christian life is serious—going under the water represents dying; joyful—splashing the water represents the glad witness to Christ's resurrection; obedient—we pledge ourselves to service; free—we exercise our liberty; being added in—we become members of the body of Christ; and full of grace—we acknowledge the abundant provisions of God.

Baptism as the Gospel Acted Out

Baptism is about the work of Jesus Christ on behalf of sinners. Jesus died on the cross, was buried, and on the third day arose in victory. Baptism reenacts this central, life-defining event in the life of Jesus Christ (Rom 6:4).

When someone who acknowledges their need to be baptized says they are afraid of the water, I say, "Good. That's the whole point." There is a primordial fear of water that is deep enough to drown in. As a new Christian looks into this deep water, he sees a place where death can close in around his head. No wonder it is a fearsome thing. But as the believer steps down into the small waves of the baptismal pool, she senses that though she goes into the watery grave, the Jesus who won the victory long ago has won it for her, and he, too, will be raised up in glad celebration that the sting of death has been removed (1 Cor 15:56-57).

No one who does not believe that Jesus is risen will want to go into these waters, for as I say to those preparing for baptism in our church, "If Jesus is not raised up, I cannot lift you up out of the water either. This is about his victory. But if there was no victory, then 'your faith is futile; you are still in your sins' (1 Cor 15:17). We are without hope; pity us for we have believed in vain. If Jesus is dead, so are we!"

Baptism as Ordination to Service

Baptism is about God's ordination of believers to service and ministry. Christ's baptism by John is the pattern for those who would "follow Christ in baptism." Though there is a good deal of discussion surrounding the meaning of John's baptism and especially what it signified for Jesus, this much is clear and generally agreed upon:

Jesus' baptism was the public announcement that God had committed Himself to do battle with sin, darkness, evil, and the devil through His Son. After his baptism Jesus "was led by the Spirit into the desert to be tempted by the devil" (Matt 4:1). The powers of darkness urged Jesus to ignore what he understood God to have called him to do in his baptism, that is, to save the world by being a suffering servant (Matt 3:17; Isa 42:1). The devil whispered, "You don't have to die for these people; feed them from these stones, and they will follow you anywhere" (see John 6:12-15). Then the devil cooed, "Jump off the temple tower and let the angels rescue you; that will prove you are the Messiah they look for." Finally, the devil purred, "Bow down and worship me, and I will release the whole world to you." Each time Jesus answered with Scripture that defended the wisdom, integrity, and holiness of God the Father (Matt 4:1-11). A Christian who rises from the water and walks out into the world goes there to defend the honor of God against the evil one who seeks to shake our pledge to follow God obediently.

The baptism of Jesus gathers the Trinity close to the scene. Here is the Son in the water, the Spirit in the dove, and the Father in the voice (Matt 3:16-17).[3] The Father's unconcealed delight is felt in this baptismal blessing as He smiles on the Son. God crowns Jesus with the royal psalm, "This is my Son, whom I love" (Ps 2:7). Jesus lived with royal dignity and power, and when he died they hung a sign for all to see, "King of the Jews!" The Father ordains him for service as the suffering servant of Isaiah's profound vision, "with him I am well pleased" (Isa 42:1). Christ's own people did not recognize him (John 1:10-11) because they were expecting a different kind of messiah. Jesus went to the cross and died an offering for the world and its sin. "We all, like sheep, have gone astray, each of us has turned to his own way; and the Lord has laid on him the iniquity of us all" (Isa 53:6).

The understanding that we are saved to serve grows out of this baptismal experience. All Christians, not only vocational ministers, are ordained for service and ministry at their baptism. I remind those who are being baptized: God smiles on you today and sends you from these waters to serve the Living Water to all those who thirst.

Baptism as Personal Testimony

Baptism is about each individual's answering the invitation to follow Jesus for him/herself. Here Baptists differ greatly from most Christians. Infant baptism is the practice among the great majority of Christians. Without trying to answer the arguments that are made for infant baptism, I simply say there is no warrant in the New Testament for baptism of anyone but believers.[4] Baptism is a sign of God's grace, but although God's grace calls us to and prepares us for salvation, we are not saved until we experience God's grace and forgiveness through believing faith. Then, and only then, are we ready for the baptism Christ commissioned his church to give (Matt 28:18-20).

When this doctrine was first recovered by the Swiss Brethren in 1525, they were ridiculed as "Wiedertaufer," or Anabaptists, and hunted down and killed by fellow Christians who abhorred the idea that their own baptism was called into question and that these heretics would not baptize their own children. But the Anabaptists persisted in believing that God's mercy is sufficient for the unbaptized child, and that no religious rite was needed to protect the little ones.[5] Furthermore, they were sure God did not want any faith that was not personally offered to God by the individual believer. You will hear Baptists say, "God has many children, but no grandchildren." We come one by one, and we come on our own, drawn to experience faith by the work of the Holy Spirit and the prayers of family and church.

Baptism as Witness to Religious Liberty

Baptism is about the liberty of every person to respond to God's Holy Spirit as he or she will. No one, not even God, coerces another into the Kingdom of God. We may pray, preach, persuade, and even urgently plead, but we must not coerce. God wants the worship of a free heart; no other offering of worship can be genuinely given. Hubmaier said, "Faith is a work of God and not of the Heretics Tower."[6] To be coerced to the water either by church domination or the unholy linkage of religion with the powers of the state is wrong, and its practice is to be exposed and resisted wherever it may be practiced.

Baptism is the free witness that "I am a believer; I belong to Jesus Christ and to no other." In baptism a Christian freely proclaims, "I take the mark of Christ upon me, I am now a part of the body of Christ, his church, and I gladly live in the midst of a dying world knowing that Christ Jesus has given resurrection and new life to all who believe."

Baptism as a Sign of Church Membership

Baptists know nothing of private baptism. This is a church matter; we call it an "ordinance." The church witnesses the believer's confession of faith; the church appoints the one to baptize on their behalf; the church gathers around to prayerfully encourage and pledge to be faithful in helping this new Christian mature in Christ.

There is a visceral bonding of believer and congregation as the one being baptized, our new brother or sister in Christ, confesses aloud, "Jesus is Lord," is buried under the water in view of the congregation, and is raised up in the victory of Christ. Baptized in this manner, the one baptized looks like a drowning victim who has been pulled from the water. Rescued by Christ's victory, the baptized believer has his/her feet placed on solid ground in the midst of the believing church. Baptism announces in the most dramatic way, "Jesus has saved you and placed you in the body of believers. We belong to one another by his lavish mercies and abundant grace."

The baptism of believers who freely confess the lordship of Christ, then, is the marvelous gift God has given Christians to remind them of their responsibility to come for themselves and their freedom to come as they are drawn by God's Spirit. It is the sign that undergirds the doctrine of the priesthood of believers, the doctrine of congregational government of the local and autonomous church, and the joyful commitment to live as Jesus lived, to walk as he walked, to live a new life (Rom 6:14).

At the heart of baptism is the public declaration that for this person, there has grown in the heart the conviction that whatever others may say, he/she will say, "Jesus is Lord," and buried with Christ in baptism, rises to walk in newness of life.

Notes

[1]William R. Estep, *The Anabaptist Story* (Nashville: Broadman Press, 1963).

[2]From 1525 to sometime around 1641, believer's baptism was done by pouring water on the head of the believer. In 1525 Balthasar Hubmaier baptized more than 300 believers out of a milkpail. [William R. Estep, *The Anabaptist Story* (Nashville: Broadman Press, 1963) 55.] In 1641 Edward Barber wrote *A Small Treatise on Baptisme or Dipping* in which he called for a recovery of "True Baptisme or Dipping Ephe. 4.5, Instituted by the Lord Jesus Christ." The First London Confession was released by seven Particular Baptist churches in London in 1644 and expressed the conviction that baptism was to be done by immersion. Article XL reads: "The way and manner of the dispensing of this Ordinance the Scripture holds out to be dipping or plunging the whole body under water: it being a signe, must answer the thing signified, which are these: first, the washing the whole soule in the bloud of Christ: Secondly, that interest the Saints have in the death, buriall, and resurrection; thirdly, together with a confirmation of our faith, that as certainly as the body is buried under water, and riseth againe, so certainly shall the bodies of the Saints be raised by the power of Christ, in the day of the resurrection, to reigne with Christ." [H. Leon McBeth, *A Sourcebook for Baptist Heritage* (Nashville: Broadman Press, 1990) 42, 50.]

[3]Frederick Dale Bruner, *The Christbook* (Waco TX: Word) 87-89.

[4]One of the earliest presentations on this question was written by Balthasar Hubmaier, *On the Christian Baptism of Believers*. In this effort Hubmaier persuasively argues that infants should not be baptized, "ten markstones which I have established . . . that all who believe are under the obligation to let themselves be baptized according to the institution of Christ." Balthasar Hubmaier, *Balthasar Hubmaier, Theologian of Anabaptism*, translated and edited by H. Wayne Pipkin and John H. Yoder, (Scottsdale: Herald Press, 1989) 129. See pp. 114-128 for the discussion.

[5]Ibid., 139-43.

[6]Ibid., 308.

A Question of Faith and a Personal Decision

—————— Karl Heinz Walter ——————

I could simply respond to the declaration "Why I am a Baptist" like this: "Because I was born into a Baptist family! I am a Baptist in the third generation." But this would be too simple a description of the situation.

I was brought up during the Nazi regime in Germany, and as a young boy was very much impressed by the propaganda and the Hitler youth movement. As a professional officer, my father served in North Africa and then was a prisoner of war in the United States. We had to leave our hometown, Hannover, because of the bombing and live in places were there was no Baptist church. Although my parents have been very much involved in Baptist life, it had no real influence on me until the end of the second world war.

One year after the end of the war I was invited to attend a boy's camp. It was familiar to me and was therefore attractive. Furthermore we had the promise of enough food, which meant a lot in a time of starvation. At that camp the Bible study on the Ten Commandments forced me to review my life. For the first time the Word of God really related to my situation. But it was more than a year before I came to a clear decision to follow Jesus. It happened when I was almost alone, with no emotional pressure from an evangelist. In many ways it was not a typical Baptist conversion, but it rooted deeply and began with a clear reorientation of my life, so that only a day later I would publicly confess my faith before the other boys at the camp. My faith came to an early test when I had to wait six months to be baptized.

Only today I realize how important is the kind of conversion we experience. As in many other questions, the beginning provides

characteristic features for the rest of our lives. This gave me an understanding of my ministry and kept me in it.

My parents always encouraged me to prove my faith in practical
deeds, that the truth I learned by myself from reading the Bible must
become relevant in my life. Very early I understood the Bible as a book
that reveals to me a way to live with God and Jesus. Only much later
did theologies become important to me. "If your faith has no influence
and relevance in your daily life, it is worth nothing." Thus was my
mother's teaching.

Besides this, it was important that at the beginning of my "Baptist
life" I met some important Baptist personalities who became early
stewards of my life. I learned from them how to read the Bible faithfully every morning. An American Baptist pastor whom I served as an
interpreter introduced me to the power and secret of effective prayer. A
former professor of the Baptist Theological Seminary in Germany, he
challenged me to use the Greek language to study the Bible in its original languages, especially the New Testament. Meeting such important
"Moses-type Baptists" meant a lot to a young Baptist.

I emphasize this because to be a Baptist in Europe and especially in
Germany means to belong to a minority. If you have never lived in a
minority situation, it is difficult to understand that to become a Baptist
is from the very beginning a *status confessionis*. You are culturally different from the majority, and you belong to a church where religion is
not a matter of a certain culture but a question of faith and a personal
decision. For me, it also had certain consequences in the lifestyle that
was different from my fellow students. It even made some friendships
difficult.

This *status confessionis* required theological argumentation. What
is the difference? Why not be like a Lutheran or Reformed Christian,
who are the majority in my country? It was not enough just to be born
into a Baptist family. The Baptist principles must become a lively part
of your own identity.

The more I studied the Bible and listened to teachings, the more I
became convinced that the Baptist theology about the church was
closer to the early church of the New Testament than I could see and
understand in other churches. When I heard the call into the ministry,

I was never uncertain about the place of serving the Lord. It would be as a Baptist pastor.

A further important influence came when I discovered the results of early "Anabaptist" studies. In the 1950s we had the first publications about the beginning of the movement from the late fifteenth and early sixteenth centuries. The International Baptist Seminary, then in Rüschlikon, Switzerland, played an important role in these studies. The state churches had always hindered studies of this period and only pointed with malicious joy to the extreme situation in Muenster, Germany. The condemnation of Anabaptists in the *Confessio Augustana* gave even more emphasis to the intention to treat Baptists as sectarian. This is still the case in many European countries and by far not overcome. But when Mennonites and Baptists during those years began to collect as many facts of this period as they could find, we got another picture. When I learned of the basic theological principles of the Anabaptists, I immediately knew that was where I belonged. These seven basic principles are:

• the Word of God as the only basis of faith and life

• the acknowledgment of Jesus Christ as the Son of God, who is the only source of salvation for all human beings

• the church as a community of believers baptized according to their personal confession of faith in Jesus Christ

• autonomy of the local church

• separation of church and state

• the basic right of all human beings to be respected in their dignity and to guarantee the freedom to choose their faith

• the obligation to help and care for other human beings in need

I understood that in consequence of these principles there was a strong commitment to fight for human rights.

Although I know there is a discussion among church historians as to whether or not the Baptist movement on the continent of Europe has any direct links with the Anabaptists of the fifteenth century, it is more than evident today that the theological links are there. In the current debates about Baptist identity in Europe, this tradition of the time of the reformation in Europe is more than helpful and gives new direction.

Throughout these reflections one can read between the lines another question that is even more relevant today: Why am I still a Baptist?

After more than forty years in the ministry as a Baptist pastor and leader, I am sometimes astonished to have survived. I am conservative in my theology and by no means a liberal in theological terms, but I don't appreciate conservative attitudes as they have been seen in recent years. I dislike categories such as conservative and liberal because they are not spiritual and biblical terms; they are instruments to classify brothers and sisters of the same faith. Regrettably, they are used to destroy the integrity of fellow believers with whom we should better talk with openness and the willingness to listen and to learn. Evangelical and conservative Christian became almost synonyms for being narrow-minded and opposing every modern development of life. It often has caused the loss of a whole generation who felt they were left alone to face their daily problems.

It has been very helpful to me personally that I never became a typical traditional Baptist. The Lord called me for half of the time of my ministry to be a youth pastor for an association, for the Baptist Union of my country, and for the Baptist World Alliance. This kept me on the move and under the permanent challenge of open and direct questions, when young people had confidence that I would listen.

At the beginning of my pilgrimage I became part of the "Rufer Movement" among German Baptists. These young people and youth pastors wanted to reach the youth of their generation. Since they did not come to us, we had to go where we could find them. This became a way of discoveries. We discovered that the disciples were sent out at least two by two, so we tried the same. We noticed that they had to leave the traditional places of service in order to preach the gospel, so we did the same. Soon we were confronted with questions we had never raised or heard before, since we came from well-protected homes. As a result, we studied our Bibles for guidance in solving current problems. In times of crisis we rediscovered the praxis of fasting and praying. Most importantly, we were trained to listen in our quiet times to the voice of Jesus.

This whole process created openness to elements of the faith that most of us had never known before, such as the charismatic movement, and taught us not to condemn because it was new and different. These are the attitudes:

- to reach the unbelieving people of our time and to be directed by this wish in all we do as church

- to listen and to be open to the questions of our time and to find answers from the Bible that open ways and means to live in the future

- to work as a team, understanding that this is the mission principle Jesus taught the disciples

- to be committed to listen to the voice of Jesus and the Father and to avoid everything that may separate us from them

I had the privilege of living my ministry according to these attitudes. This is the main reason why I am still a Baptist.

Today I notice that many pastors feel burned out. It becomes almost a syndrome of Baptist ministers. There are many reasons for this. Many are forced to work and act not according to their God-given gifts, but are pushed by the expectations of the members of the church and treated like an employee in any other business. This is not fair and is not what the Bible tells us.

I am still a Baptist because I had the chance to conduct my pastorate always in a team that tried to understand the will of God. The system in German churches to have active elders who are laypersons can also be difficult, because we can be very difficult as personalities. But I had the luck to be in creative teams that allowed me to work according to my gifts. Of course, there were always many things I had to do in other jobs. Nevertheless, there was space to serve with my gifts, which affords satisfaction and makes the work easier. This recognition and appreciation of gifts liberates the power of creativity. Without creativity there is no ministry in the Kingdom. Creativity is one of the characteristics of the Holy Spirit. Without it we will not be able to face the problems and challenges inside and outside the churches.

Many Baptist churches around the world have developed a tendency to overemphasize their own situations. If they lose their mission to the world, they will soon die. But the knowledge of what is happening around the world is very little. The majority of Baptist churches have a very small radius of concern. This is dangerous, and at the same time those churches miss all the excitement of what God is doing.

When I stood for the first time in the deep Jordan valley at the Sea of Galilee, I became suddenly aware of what Jesus really did when he sent the disciples over the mountains of Judea into the whole world. He led them out of the very narrow perspective of the Jordan valley with no real horizon and put their feet on a worldwide field. From its beginning the church was a world church.

Baptists were among the first to form a worldwide organization of churches. The Baptist World Alliance has kept my eyes open to the world and given me the opportunity to serve around the world. This confirmed my trust that God has an important place for Baptists. It hurts me when Baptists speak negatively and destructively of Baptist churches. This is not the proper response to God's plans. How often I have wished I could bring Baptist churches from places of frustration due to small results of their mission to places of an awakening.

In thinking of Baptist churches around the world, I dream of a situation where it will be possible for all to share with each other what God is doing. This would afford great inspiration and encouragement. I also dream of a situation where we as Baptists stop radically categorizing each other and placing us in boxes labeled with unbiblical and discriminating descriptions.

There is a world waiting for the church to become a clear instrument of the grace of God that we and our forebears have received in order to grant this mercy in His name to the world.

Contributors

Jimmy R. Allen, Th.D., President of JRA Consulting, Inc., and Chaplain of Big Canoe Chapel, holds degrees from Howard Payne University and Southwestern Baptist Theological Seminary. He served as pastor of First Baptist Church, San Antonio, Texas, and as president of the Southern Baptist Convention. As CEO of the Radio and Television Commission of the Southern Baptist Convention, he founded the ACTS Cable Network. For eight years he hosted *Life Today* on national cable TV. He was also producer of the Emmy Award-winning 1968-TV program "China: Walls and Bridges." His book, *Burden of a Secret: A Story of Truth and Mercy in a Family Faced with AIDS*, examines the lessons learned from grief and dying. As co-author of *Bridging the Gap*, a report on news media and religion in America, he won the Special Wilbur Award.

Robert C. Ballance, Jr., D.Min., Executive Editor of *Baptists Today*, holds degrees from Mars Hill College, Southeastern Baptist Theological Seminary, Drew University, and North Carolina State University. He has served as pastor of churches in North Carolina and Texas, and is a member of the Academy of Parish Clergy and the Alban Institute. His writings have been published in *Pulpit Digest, Biblical Recorder, New Horizons in Adult Education, The Clergy Journal,* and Smyth & Helwys devotional literature and Bible study curriculum. His extensive involvement in church and community service projects includes participation in projects around the country and in Puerto Rico, Czechoslovakia, and Germany. His avocations are jogging, writing, story-collecting/telling, travel, Internet-surfing, and hands-on mission work.

Tony Campolo, Ph.D., Professor of Sociology at Eastern College in St. Davids, Pennsylvania, is founder and president of the Evangelical Association for the Promotion of Education (EAPE/Kingdomworks), a ministry that serves at-risk youth in urban America and sponsors education and economic development programs in third world countries.

Campolo is the author of twenty-six books and hosts a weekly television program, *Hashing It Out,* on the Odyssey Network. He is an ordained minister and serves as associate pastor of Mount Carmel Baptist Church in West Philadelphia. He and his wife Peggy take great pride in their two children and three grandchildren.

Jimmy Carter (James Earl Carter, Jr.), a native of Plains, Georgia, and 39th President of the United States, is a graduate of the U.S. Naval Academy and served as a Navy lieutenant under Admiral Hyman Rickover in the development of the nuclear submarine program. Elected as Georgia's 76th Governor in 1971, he won the presidential nomination on the first ballot at the 1976 Democratic National Convention and was elected in November. During his term as President he achieved notable progress in foreign policy, human rights, and domestic programs. In 1982 he was named distinguished professor at Emory University in Atlanta. He founded the Carter Center, dedicated in 1996, which addresses national and international issues of public policy. The author of fifteen books, he teaches Sunday School regularly at Maranatha Baptist Church in Plains, and he and Mrs. Carter are longtime Habitat for Humanity volunteers.

Carolyn Weatherford Crumpler, M.R.E., born in Mississippi and reared in Florida, became a Christian and joined the Baptist church in 1943. She holds degrees from Florida State University and New Orleans Baptist Theological Seminary, where she received the Distinguished Alumnus Award. Following a career as a librarian, she was promotion director of the Alabama Woman's Missionary Union and executive director of the Florida and Southern Baptist Convention WMUs. She served eight years with the Baptist Joint Committee and the Southern Baptist Foundation, ten years on the Baptist World Alliance General Council and Executive Committee, and is a founding member of the Baptist Center for Ethics. Current service includes Lydia's House, American Bible Society, God's Home for Families, and Friends of New Churches.

James C. Denison, Ph.D., Pastor of Park Cities Baptist Church, Dallas, Texas, holds degrees from Houston Baptist University, where he was named Distinguished Alumnus, and Southwestern Baptist Theological Seminary. Except for four years spent at Second-Ponce de Leon Baptist Church in Atlanta, Georgia, his entire ministry has been in Texas. He has served as teaching fellow and instructor of philosophy of religion at Southwestern Seminary and as adjunct professor at McAfee School of Theology of Mercer University in Atlanta. He is the author of *Seven Crucial Questions about the Bible, Life on the Brick Pile*, and *The Apostolic Church* (forthcoming). He has served as a trustee of Howard Payne University and Mercer University and as a member of the Advisory Board of Truett Theological Seminary.

James M. Dunn, Ph.D., Executive Director of the Baptist Joint Committee on Public Affairs in Washington since 1981, is now a faculty member of the divinity school at Wake Forest University in Winston-Salem, North Carolina. A native Texan, he holds degrees from Texas Wesleyan College, Southwestern Baptist Theological Seminary, and the London School of Economics and Political Science. He has appeared on all the major network television news programs, including *The Today Show* and *Nightline*, and has served as president of Bread for the World and chairman of the Ethics Commission of the Baptist World Alliance. He is co-author of *Politics: A Guidebook for Christians, Endangered Species, Roots of Hope, An Approach to Christian Ethics, Equal Separation, The Fundamentalist Phenomenon*, and *Teacher Renewal*.

Jocelyn L. Foy, M.S., Licensed Minister of First Baptist Church, American Baptist Conference, Winston-Salem, North Carolina, and director of the adult education program at Greensboro College, holds degrees from the University of North Carolina/Greensboro and North Carolina A&T State University. She takes great pride in her profession as a third-generation educator and lifelong learner. Her various career administrative positions have enabled her to interact with and serve as spiritual mentor to thousands of students and staff members. Her current goal is to become a member of the charter class in the Master of

Divinity program in the Divinity School at Wake Forest University. Her vocational goal is to serve as a chaplain in an ecumenical college environment and to pursue ordination as a Baptist clergy.

Carole "Kate" Harvey, M.Div., Executive Director of the Ministers Council, Valley Forge, Pennsylvania, holds degrees from State University of New York/Albany, University of Cincinnati, and Andover Newton Theological School and is currently pursuing the Doctor of Ministry degree at Hartford Seminary. Her career has included secondary and college teaching and pastorates in Rhode Island. She has served as editor of *Minister* and as Ministerial Leadership Commission Chair for the American Baptist Church, USA. Community service includes membership in the National Religious Leaders Program and on the Rhode Island State Senate Ethics Committee. Her sermons have been published in *Proclaiming the Vision: The Priesthood of All Believers*, *The Sermon on the Mount*, and *Sermons Seldom Heard*.

Brian Haymes, Ph.D., Principal of Bristol Baptist College, where he prepared for the ministry, holds degrees from the University of Bristol and the University of Exeter in Great Britain. His doctoral thesis, *The Concept of the Knowledge of God*, was published by St. Martin's Press. He has been pastor of churches in Bristol, Exeter, and Nottingham; has served as tutor and principal of Northern Baptist College in Manchester; and has taught Christian ethics. His current research interests include theological ethics, homiletics, and Baptist principles. From 1993 to 1994 he was president of the Baptist Union of Great Britain. He and his wife Jenny are rejoicing in the birth of their first grandson.

Margaret (Meg) B. Hess, D.Min., a native of Danville, Virginia, is in her eighth year as pastor of First Baptist Church, Nashua, New Hampshire. She holds degrees from Meredith College and Andover Newton Theological School. Ordained by First Baptist Church in Newton, Massachusetts, she served pastorates in that area for ten years. Since 1983 she has taught preaching as an adjunct faculty member at Andover Newton. A member-associate with the American Association of Pastoral Counselors, she has a private practice as a pastoral psychotherapist at the Emmaus Institute in Nashua.

Bill J. Leonard, Ph.D., Charter Dean of Wake Forest University Divinity School, holds degrees from Texas Wesleyan University and Boston University and did postdoctoral study at Yale University. He has served as chair of the department of religion and philosophy at Samford University, Birmingham, Alabama; as professor of church history at the Southern Baptist Theological Seminary, Louisville, Kentucky; and as visiting professor at Seinan Gakuin University in Japan. He is the author of twelve books and is a frequent contributor to a number of periodicals and journals, including *Christian Century.* He is currently writing a new history of Baptists and recently co-edited the *Encyclopedia of Religious Controversies.* In recent years he has received or participated in nine grants from various foundations.

Molly T. Marshall, Ph.D., Professor of Theology and Spiritual Formation at Central Baptist Theological Seminary in Kansas City, Kansas, is a native of Oklahoma, and holds degrees from Oklahoma Baptist University, the University of Oklahoma, and the Southern Baptist Theological Seminary. She was ordained by St. Matthews Baptist Church in Louisville, Kentucky, and was pastor of Jordan Baptist Church in Eagle Station, Kentucky. She served as professor and associate dean of the School of Theology at Southern Seminary, where she received the Findley and Louvenia Edge Faculty Teaching Award in 1993. She was adjunct professor of religion at Ottawa University, was extended the privilege of call from American Baptist Churches in 1997, and is the author of two books, *No Salvation Outside the Church?* and *What It Means To Be Human.*

Emmanuel L. McCall, Sr., D.Min., a native of Pennsylvania, is founder and pastor of Christian Fellowship Baptist Church in Atlanta, Georgia. He holds degrees from the University of Louisville, The Southern Baptist Theological Seminary, and Emory University. He served on the executive staff of the Southern Baptist Convention Home Mission Board and was pastor of 28th Street Baptist Church in Louisville, president of the Kentucky State Baptist Congress and of the national alumni association of Southern Seminary, a trustee of Atlanta University Center, and a visiting professor at seminaries in Ghana, Liberia, and Nigeria in West Africa. He is chair of the Ethics Commission of the Baptist World Alliance and adjunct professor of spiritual formations at the McAfee School of Theology of Mercer University in Atlanta.

Gary Parker, Ph.D., Coordinator for Baptist Principles at Cooperative Baptist Fellowship in Atlanta, Georgia, holds degrees from Furman University, Southeastern Baptist Theological Seminary, and Baylor University. He has served as pastor of churches in North and South Carolina, Texas, and Missouri. His teaching experience includes lectures at Southeastern Seminary, Baylor University, and Eden Theological Seminary. He has been a preacher and worship leader for national and international conferences and a speaker for writers conferences. He is the author of four fiction books, four non-fiction books, and numerous articles published in a variety of magazines and Bible study materials. His personal interests include long-distance biking, writing, and golf.

R. Keith Parks, Th.D., immediate past Global Missions Coordinator for the Cooperative Baptist Fellowship in Atlanta, Georgia, is a native of Tennessee and holds degrees from North Texas State University and Southwestern Baptist Theological Seminary. Prior service includes the pastorate of Red Springs Baptist Church and instructor in religion at Hardin-Simmons University, both in Texas. During three terms as a missionary in Indonesia, he taught and served as president of the Baptist Theological Seminary. For twelve years he was president of the Mission Support Division of the Foreign Mission Board of the Southern Baptist Convention. He has been presented a number of honorary degrees and awards from colleges across the country. He is the author of *Crosscurrents* and *World in View*, a part of the AD 2000 Series published by New Hope Press.

James M. Pitts, D.Min., Chaplain and Associate Professor of Religion at Furman University in Greenville, South Carolina, is a native of Washington, D.C., and holds degrees from Furman University, Southeastern Baptist Theological Seminary, and The Southern Baptist Theological Seminary. He has served as pastoral counselor in congregational and hospital settings, specializing in crisis counseling, substance abuse intervention, and career guidance for persons in ministry. He received the Lewis W. Newman Award for lifelong leadership in career clarification for ministry. His sermons and essays have been published in a number of books and journals. He is Chairman of the Board of Smyth & Helwys Publishing, Inc., a publisher of educational resources and Christian books.

Charles E. Poole, M.Div., a native of Macon, Georgia, and Pastor of Northminster Baptist Church in Jackson, Mississippi, holds degrees from Macon College, Mercer University, and Southeastern Baptist Theological Seminary. His previous pastorates include the First Baptist Churches of Washington, D.C., and Macon, Georgia, and associate pastor of Highland Hills Baptist Church in Macon. He has served as a trustee of Mercer University and received the honorary Doctor of Divinity degree and the Louie D. Newton Award for outstanding service to the University. He is the author of four books, *Don't Cry Past Tuesday*, *Is Life Fair?*, *The Tug of Home*, and *Beyond the Broken Lights* (forthcoming), and his articles and chapters have been published in a number of books and periodicals.

John Thomas Porter, M.Div., Pastor of Sixth Avenue Baptist Church, Birmingham, Alabama, holds degrees from Alabama State University and Morehouse College and was a 1993 Merrill Fellow at Harvard University. He was awarded the honorary Doctor of Divinity degree by Daniel Payne College and Miles College in Birmingham. He has been pastor of First Institutional Baptist Church in Detroit, Michigan, and a member of the Alabama House of Representatives and the Alabama State Board of Pardon and Parole. He has served as a trustee of several colleges, universities, and civic and religious organizations. He received the Brotherhood Award from the National Conference of Christians and Jews and the Alpha Phi Alpha Fraternity President's Award.

Nancy Hastings Sehested, M.Div, pastor, teacher, retreat leader, and storyteller, has been an ordained Baptist minister for twenty years and is currently pastor of Sweet Fellowship Baptist Church in Clyde, North

Carolina. She holds degrees from City College of New York and Union Theological Seminary. She was a founding member of Southern Baptist Women in Ministry in 1983 and has served as president of the Alliance of Baptists and as a member of the Board of Trustees of Central Baptist Theological Seminary in Kansas. Her essays and articles have been published in a number of journals and books, and she has appeared on television programs such as Bill Moyers' *Special Series on Religion*, and *Sword and Spirit*, co-produced by British Broadcasting Corporation. Her husband Ken Sehested is president of Baptist Peace Fellowship.

Cecil E. Sherman, Ph.D., a native of Fort Worth, Texas, was baptized as a child by Baker James Cauthen, his pastor at Polytechnic Baptist Church. He holds degrees from Baylor University, Southwestern Baptist Theological Seminary, and Princeton Theological Seminary. He has served as pastor of First Baptist Church, Chamblee, Georgia; College Station, Texas; and Asheville, North Carolina. His last full-time pastorate was Broadway Baptist Church, Fort Worth, Texas. For four years he was the charter Coordinator of the Cooperative Baptist Fellowship in Atlanta, Georgia. In semi-retirement he holds the Chair of Practical Studies at Baptist Theological Seminary in Richmond, Virginia, writes Adult *Formations* Commentary for Smyth & Helwys Publishing, and preaches most Sundays.

Walter B. Shurden, Th.D., a native of Mississippi, and Callaway Professor of Christianity and Department Chair at Mercer University, Macon, Georgia, holds degrees from Mississippi College and The Southern Baptist Theological Seminary. He has held faculty positions at McMaster Divinity College, Carson-Newman College, and Southern Seminary. He is the author of five books and the editor of seven. He has served as president of the National Association of Baptist Professors of Religion and the Historical Commission of the Southern Baptist Convention and as a member of the first steering committee of Cooperative Baptist Fellowship. He has held a pastorate in Louisiana, a professorship at Carson-Newman College, and was professor of church history and Dean of the School of Theology at Southern Seminary.

Cecil P. Staton, Jr., D.Phil., a native of Greenville, South Carolina, and President and Publisher of Smyth & Helwys Publishing, Inc., is Associate Provost for Academic Publications and associate professor in the College of Liberal Arts at Mercer University in Macon, Georgia. He holds degrees from Furman University, Southeastern Baptist Theological Seminary, and the University of Oxford, Regent's Park College, England. His prior experience includes a term as Old Testament lecturer at Oxford and two years as assistant professor of Christianity at Brewton-Parker College in Mt. Vernon, Georgia. He is the author and editor of three books, *Interpreting Amos/ Hosea/Isaiah for Preaching and Teaching*, co-editor of the series *Studies in Old Testament Interpretation*, and chair of the editorial board for *Mercer Library of Biblical Studies.*

Charles Frank "T" Thomas, M.Div., a native of Atlanta, Georgia, is international coordinator and team leader for Cooperative Baptist Fellowship work among Romanies (Gypsies), currently serving in Paris, France. He holds degrees from Furman University and Southeastern Baptist Theological Seminary. He has served as associate pastor of Salem Baptist Church in Apex, North Carolina, as a church planter in Burkina Faso and France from 1974 to 1992, and as a seminary professor in Romania. In 1992 he and his wife were appointed as the first missionaries sent out by the Cooperative Baptist Fellowship. He has studied advanced French at the University of Poitiers/Tours and advanced Romanian at the University of Paris /La Sorbonne.

Daniel Vestal, Th.D., a native of Waco, Texas, and Coordinator of the Cooperative Baptist Fellowship based in Atlanta, holds degrees from Baylor University and Southwestern Baptist Theological Seminary. He has held pastorates in Atlanta, Georgia, and in Houston, Midland, Fort Worth, and Arlington, Texas. He was founding chairman of the Board of Trustees at Truett Seminary of Baylor University, first moderator of the Cooperative Baptist Fellowship, and twice was nominated for the presidency of the Southern Baptist Convention. His board memberships include the Baptist General Convention of Texas, Mexican Baptist Bible Institute, and Southern Baptist Peace Committee. He is the author of *Pulling Together* and *The Doctrine of Creation.*

Charles R. Wade, Th.D., Pastor of First Baptist Church of Arlington, Texas since 1976, began preaching at age fifteen and has served churches in Oklahoma, Germany, and Texas. He holds degrees from Oklahoma Baptist University and Southwestern Baptist Theological Seminary. His doctoral dissertation, *Black Theology: An Attempt at White Understanding*, led to leadership in interracial ministry and community service. He recently completed his second term as president of the Baptist General Convention of Texas. In 1986 First Baptist Church began Mission Arlington, a comprehensive outreach ministry including Bible studies, provision of needs, employment opportunities, transportation, and counseling services. In this ministry 400 volunteers reach 5,000 people each Sunday. The church seeks to live its motto: "A Family of Faith . . . Caring for You."

Karl Heinz Walter, a native of Hannover, Germany, is general secretary of the European Baptist Federation and regional secretary of the Baptist World Alliance for Europe. Following the pursuit of vocational training as an insurance merchant, he engaged in study at the Theological Seminary of the German Baptist in Hamburg. From there he progressed to studies in theology, soziopsychology, and pedagogy at the University of Hamburg. Following service as pastor of the Baptist Church in Minden, he was director of the Baptist Youth Department of Germany West, and chairman of European Baptist Youth and of the Youth Committee of the Baptist World Alliance. He later served as pastor of the Baptist church in Bremerhaven. He holds the honorary Doctor of Divinity degree from Furman University in Greenville, South Carolina.